Fashion Writing

Acting as a comprehensive primer for the field of fashion writing, this book provides an accessible entry point for readers from diverse backgrounds, giving them a clear understanding of the intricacies of fashion writing, the outlets in which it appears, and the possibilities beyond the page.

Fashion Writing: A Primer lays out a framework for various types of fashion writing (runway and trend reports, service pieces, features, and more) while offering students a solid foundation of fashion history, cultural touchstones, common fashion terminology, and contemporary issues affecting the fashion industry today. Featuring interviews with current fashion journalists, such as Robin Givhan, Sarah Mower, Charlie Porter, and Amanda Winnie Kabuiku, as well as annotated bibliographies centred on the themes of each chapter, this book delivers fashion writing essentials for anyone interested in the field. Readers will come away aware of the many influences on the fashion world, helping them establish credibility as a fashion writer.

Covering both print and online outlets, this is a valuable text for students with an interest in fashion communication, journalism, and fashion media, as well as early career fashion professionals looking for a complete guide to the industry.

Claudia B. Manley has been a university lecturer for over 15 years at Western University in London, Ontario (Canada) and has published in both fashion writing and literary fiction.

Abi Slone is an editor and writer whose credits include *The Globe and Mail*, *Architectural Digest*, and the CBC and curating the Isabella Blow and Daphne Guinness fashion installation, "Fashion Blows."

Fashion Writing
A Primer

Claudia B. Manley with Abi Slone

LONDON AND NEW YORK

Cover image: © Getty Images

First published 2023
by Routledge
4 Park Square, Milton Park, Abingdon, Oxon OX14 4RN

and by Routledge
605 Third Avenue, New York, NY 10158

Routledge is an imprint of the Taylor & Francis Group, an informa business

© 2023 Claudia B. Manley and Abi Slone

The right of Claudia B. Manley and Abi Slone to be identified as authors of this work has been asserted in accordance with sections 77 and 78 of the Copyright, Designs and Patents Act 1988.

All rights reserved. No part of this book may be reprinted or reproduced or utilised in any form or by any electronic, mechanical, or other means, now known or hereafter invented, including photocopying and recording, or in any information storage or retrieval system, without permission in writing from the publishers.

Trademark notice: Product or corporate names may be trademarks or registered trademarks, and are used only for identification and explanation without intent to infringe.

British Library Cataloguing-in-Publication Data
A catalogue record for this book is available from the British Library

Library of Congress Cataloging-in-Publication Data
Names: Manley, Claudia B., author. | Slone, Abigail, 1972– author.
Title: Fashion writing : a primer / Claudia B. Manley with Abigail Slone.
Description: Abingdon, Oxon ; New York, NY : Routledge, 2023. | Includes bibliographical references and index.
Identifiers: LCCN 2022025196 | ISBN 9780367498450 (hardback) | ISBN 9780367498436 (paperback) | ISBN 9781003047629 (ebook)
Subjects: LCSH: Fashion writing.
Classification: LCC TT503.5 .M35 2023 | DDC 808.06/674692—dc23/eng/20220819
LC record available at https://lccn.loc.gov/2022025196

ISBN: 978-0-367-49845-0 (hbk)
ISBN: 978-0-367-49843-6 (pbk)
ISBN: 978-1-003-04762-9 (ebk)

DOI: 10.4324/9781003047629

Typeset in Goudy
by Apex CoVantage, LLC

For my mother, my first instructor in style

Contents

List of Tables viii
List of Figures ix
Acknowledgements x

Introduction 1

SECTION 1
Foundational Knowledge 11

1 Where Did You Get That Outfit? A Brief History of Fashion 13
2 It's All in the Details: The Language of Fashion 30
3 The Write Stuff: Writing Basics 67

SECTION 2
Working It 79

4 Ready for Take-off: The Runway Report 81
5 Don't Get Left Behind: Trend Reports and Service Pieces 96
6 Do You See What I See? Fashion Beyond Fashion 110

SECTION 3
Broadening Your Focus 127

7 Taking It All In: Contemporary Issues in Fashion 129
8 Pitch, Please 148

Postgraduate Programmes in Fashion Communication 157
Index 164

Tables

3.1 Guide to Digital Platforms   73

Figures

2.1	Culottes	34
2.2	Fit and flare as seen in Dior's New Look	38
2.3	Mandarin collar	40
2.4	Batwing sleeve	41
2.5	Herringbone	43
2.6	Seersucker suit	45
2.7	Godet pleats	50
2.8	Peplum	51
2.9	Bellow pocket versus patch pocket	52
2.10	Brogues	55
5.1	Trend Pyramid	101

Acknowledgements

Thank you to my editors at Routledge, Margaret Farrelly and Elizabeth Cox, as well as the editorial assistants, Priscille Biehlmann and Hannah McKeating, for their guidance throughout this process. Thank you also to all who agreed to be interviewed and shared their experience and expertise. In addition, debts of gratitude are owed to Abi Slone for her interviews, work on Chapters 2 and 5, and early feedback on this book, Jill DiDonato for her feedback and editorial eye, and J. Burbage for her work on the bibliography.

I would like to thank my family for their support – my partner, Liss Platt, and our son Ian Manley, and my parents, John and Angelika Manley. I am thankful to Kathleen Fraser, director of the Writing Program at Western University in London, Ontario, for suggesting I design the course upon which this book is based; however, this book would not have crossed my mind had it not been for the suggestion by Mo Angelos. I'm glad I took your advice! Thank you to Gayle Billat and Sharlene Goings of the Yarniacs podcast for sharing their expertise and Ana Lucía Sarmiento for her translation of the Government of Mexico press release. Many thanks go to Cal Biurk, Ciara Brennan, Susan Fast, Gail Leger, Edith Milton, and Céline Sibley who all graciously read excerpts and provided feedback, and last but not least, to all my friends who listened to me over the course of this book and provided support, feedback, and inspiration.

Introduction

Have you ever told someone you wanted to pursue fashion writing, only to be greeted with something along the lines of, "Is that really a thing?" Creative writing, which encompasses fiction, poetry, and creative nonfiction, is generally understood and accepted, but fashion writing seems too easily dismissed.

The genre can also mystify those who are passionately interested in fashion. How hard can it be? Aren't you simply describing clothes? Yet if you've ever tried to capture an outfit in words only to discover your listener has envisioned something entirely different, you begin to understand that it might not be that simple at all. That's because fashion writing (as a genre) is multidisciplinary, drawing on fundamentals of compelling prose.

Successful fashion writing utilizes a variety of journalistic and literary techniques. And if it's good, it positions fashion within a context – historical, cultural, or political – illuminating the power of what we choose to wear. It integrates perspectives from fields such as textile design, art history, and theatre to provide richly textured insights.

As you will see throughout this book, fashion doesn't simply spring from the mind of the designer but from a complex interplay of elements, which is called the zeitgeist. The zeitgeist is that invisible essence of an era that we unconsciously sense but take for granted. Translated as "the spirit of the times," the zeitgeist can be seen as a distillation of what is preoccupying the collective conscience of the world. This is communicated through art, movies, music, fashion, and more. When you see a certain garment, for example, you may also suddenly be able to tap into a soundtrack of that time. Elements you might think of having nothing to do with fashion – like politics or economics – also make their impact felt because they, too, contribute to the zeitgeist.

Alexander McQueen's S/S04 show, *Deliverance*, is a great example of the way fashion shows themselves refer to history and popular culture. This runway show references the 1969 Sydney Pollack film, *They Shoot Horses, Don't They?* The film's main set is a Depression-era dance marathon, where people desperately try to win a cash prize. In the following excerpt from a review, you can see how writer Sarah Mower has not only provided the context of the show but also used it to describe the clothes themselves.

DOI: 10.4324/9781003047629-1

2 Introduction

> *In the opening scene, the girls entered – dancing for all they were worth on the arms of muscle-bound sailors and hunky hopefuls – dressed in fishtailed silver lamé, figure-hugging cha-cha dresses, and show-stopping gowns with spangled bodices and huge feathered skirts. Other competitors whirled on wearing pink corseted tulle tutus over gray ballet sweats; mint satin tap-suits; or a slinky confection of gray checkerboard chiffon. A Billie Holiday look-alike, dramatically vamping in pink charmeuse and ostrich, vied for attention as flashy bodysuited showgirls were energetically twirled aloft by their partners.*
>
> – Alexander McQueen SS2004, Sarah Mower[1]

More and more, we're seeing an awareness of fashion permeate various aspects of contemporary life. Discussions that focus on how heads of state dress for functions are often contextualized within their policies and agendas and how that is reflected in what they choose to wear. Witness Michelle Obama's embrace of American designers including Jason Wu and Tracy Reese and mainstream brands such as J. Crew, the examination of what Canadian prime minister Justin Trudeau and his family wore on a visit to India, or even the potential diplomatic lapse when the Finnish minister of transport and communications Anne Berger greeted Chinese president Xi Jinping in a bright orange coat, a colour associated with Tibet.

Good fashion writing elucidates the dynamic relationship between fashion and the zeitgeist. For example, the state of the economy has been interpreted through fashion. The length of hemlines has frequently been seen as an economic indicator. The theory, put forth by economist George Taylor in 1926, suggests that the rise of hemlines indicated a rise in the stock market; since then, there has been some quantitative analysis done, which has shown, however, that while there might be a correlation, it's that hemlines reflect stock prices and not the other way around. In general, hemlines, and fashion in general, reflect more than just economics. You will see that politics, pandemics, and social movements also impact fashion.

What Is Fashion Writing?

We've told you a little about what fashion writing can do, but what constitutes fashion writing? What we will show you in *Fashion Writing: A Primer* is how diverse fashion writing can be. From catalogue copy to editorials to short stories, there are all kinds of outlets for good fashion writing. Our goal is to familiarize you with some of the ways to employ fashion writing, which at its very core contains the ability to communicate about and through clothing.

Fashion Editorial in Print

Despite the talk of the death of print, magazines such as *Elle* and *Vogue* publish editions in countries around the world including China, the Ivory Coast, and Croatia. The market for independent magazines demonstrates that fashion magazines are expanding their focus and that there are a broad range of interests that now fall under the subject heading "fashion." With this comes an acknowledgement that those interested in fashion are no longer just the stereotypical "fashionista" – generally thought of as young, white, and thin. *Renaissance* magazine, for example, understands that a love of fashion doesn't age out. Using only models who are over 40, *Renaissance* provides a space for older women to see themselves in the clothing that graces the runway.

Love magazine, part of the Conde Nast family of publications, features a more youthful but gritty experience for the fashion reader. The biannual magazine reflects many of the concerns and interests of contemporary readers. In addition to interviews with fashion celebrities and designers and runway reviews, features on queer youth movements, diversity in fashion, and reviews of books and films demonstrate the broader concerns of their readers.

Exquisite Magazine is just one of the current fashion magazines from Nigeria. Capitalizing on the vibrant African fashion scene, *Exquisite* not only features regional designers and fashion shows but also places them within the context of the international fashion world.

All these examples demonstrate not only the continued viability of print publications but also the diversity of subjects on which to write. Fashion editorial serves as a form of cultural critique, and the fashion magazine, in particular, curates trends and gives them a physical (and shoppable) form: our wardrobe or what to wear. Additionally, these magazines have online and social media presence, which multiplies the platforms where one can publish.

Beyond specifically fashion-focused publications, fashion can serve as a lens for other subjects in news and culture periodicals. Stories that have appeared in magazines and newspapers such as *The Atlantic* and *The Guardian* have used a focus on fashion to discuss other issues. *The Economist* published an invited essay on the significance for one Afghani woman of being freed from having to wear a burqa.[2] While the piece ostensibly seems to be about a garment, it uses the burqa to discuss issues of women's rights and self-determination. The 2020 inauguration of US president Joe Biden inspired numerous articles about the significance of the fashions on display that day, relating them to the political climate of the world at the time. A year later, the failed insurrection offered another opportunity to talk about clothing in a political arena. One such article for the *HuffPost* spoke to the weaponization of clothing exemplified that day.[3] Writing about fashion can provide us with a way of understanding current events and the world at large.

The Reach of the Internet

Publications that have moved from print to a web-based presence, such as *Glamour* whose final print issue was the January 2019 issue, or were designed solely for the internet, such as *Global Garbs*, reach audiences in diverse countries and underscore the continued interest in and call for solid fashion journalism.

Digital fashion editorials – web-based fashion sources that serve up viral content and are designed to be shared and engage with a large audience – are more and more prevalent. Digital is a prized medium for fashion because it delivers visual information quickly. Wondering who wore what to the Met Gala? Check your Instagram feed where fashion journalists and users alike post on-the-ground photos.

Digital fashion media can also be anti-establishment and offer an alternative look at the fashion industry. Social media accounts are editorially curated, like Diet Prada, which acts like a whistle-blower to mainstream fashion editorial. They are also written and visually curated with insider fashion language as a homage to the fashion magazine, like *Every Outfit on Sex & the City*, which is also a podcast. In either case, digital fashion writing can be considered as an alternative to print magazines, but it requires many of the same skills and a working knowledge of the formula of the genre. Social media makes the publishing process more democratic and fluid than traditional media fashion magazines. So this shift is important to note.

Spreading the Brand

Content marketing by fashion brands and retailers provides yet another arena in which to publish. This growing field builds upon digital fashion editorials and makes use of social media, blogs, apps, and services such as YouTube to reach a wider audience. By uploading content across multiple platforms, brands and retailers can stay in the forefront of consumers' minds and influence buying decisions.

As a content marketing writer, you may be asked to write an Instagram post, a weekly newsletter to subscribers, or a blog post for the company's website. Brands such as Madewell, H&M, and Tiffany & Co. all have shoppable content in their Instagram feeds. Chanel, Dior, Versace, and others have YouTube channels that feature fashion films that showcase the current collection, interviews with industry insiders, or product tutorials. All these materials require solid fashion writing skills.

In addition, a number of retailers, such as Net-a-Porter, Asos, Aïshti, and SSense, produce their own stand-alone magazines. These combine features on their products along with other articles expected in a fashion magazine such as profiles, reviews, and additional culturally relevant content.

Changing Landscapes

These discussions take place on a global scale now: the flow of information and the speed of it have increased. Understanding how to craft a piece that not only responds to the current zeitgeist but also understands its audience can make the difference between being published or not.

Dovetailing with this broader understanding of the role of fashion is a change in how people work. More and more of us are piecing together different kinds of employment, which is often referred to as a "gig economy" in North America. Of course, the internet and the rise of social media platforms have aided this. It seems that one no longer necessarily needs to have a degree in a specific discipline in order to work in that area. This has been commonly true of fashion writing as fashion journalism has predominantly been taught at art and fashion institutes. Many of the most successful fashion writers have degrees in other disciplines such as classics (Nathalie Atkinson), history (Suzy Menkes and Susanna Lau), and economics (Lynn Yaeger).

What's Inside?

This book is meant to be accessible to writers from diverse educational backgrounds and will reflect a wide range of sociopolitical, geographic, and racial perspectives. Most fashion writing textbooks have been designed for fashion or journalism students and either assume a common knowledge (specific to the field) or go beyond what an initial interest might warrant. What we offer here is an introduction to fashion writing and a platform from which to spring for those interested in furthering their studies, along with a strong foundation from which to build.

Fashion Writing: A Primer is divided into three main sections that build upon each other. With each chapter we've provided a brief annotated bibliography to help you further feed your interest. Additionally, you'll find sidebars interspersed, which explicate cultural touchstones frequently referred to and/or understood by writers, such as the significance of the movie *Annie Hall* to Ralph Lauren's career and the menswear trend of the late '70s or the recurring appeal of *The Great Gatsby* to the fashion world.

In the first section, readers will be provided with the tools to build a solid foundation. We'll start by providing some basic fashion history to level the playing field. We'll discuss "the first fashion designer" – Charles Worth and the significance of designers such as Paul Poiret, Coco Chanel, and Christian Dior as well as sketch out key eras and highlight their designers and associated looks to provide you with references you can draw upon in your reviews.

Every field has its own vocabulary and terminology, and fashion is no different. You'll be introduced to basic construction terms, different kinds of fabrics and their qualities, and definitions of cuts and styles. Being fluent in these helps establish your credibility as a fashion writer.

You could think of Chapter 3 as the "fundamentals for successful writing" chapter. The techniques discussed here apply not only to fashion writing but also to writing in general and will add a level of sophistication and finesse to your prose.

With a solid base established, it's time to move into the second section and a look at the most common forms of fashion writing: runway reports and trend report and service pieces. You'll get detailed information on how to craft your specific piece of fashion writing, and we'll provide tips on how to tailor your piece for print as well as for online publication. We'll also include brief interviews with fashion journalists discussing their journeys as well as why they chose fashion as their subject.

Section 3 touches on other ways fashion might be utilized in writing. Starting with using fashion as a lens – whether in journalism or creative writing – you'll understand how fashion can be employed to speak to ideas off the runway. For example, clothing has been used as a pivotal plot point as in William Gibson's *Zero*

History, as cultural criticism such as the work of Pulitzer Prize–winning fashion journalist Robin Givhan, or as a way to map emotional or psychological journeys as the book and play *Love, Loss, and What I Wore* did.

We also highlight contemporary issues and discussions in the world of fashion so readers are well-informed, such as the slow fashion movement and questions about cultural appropriation. Being a fashion writer entails knowing about more than clothes; a good fashion writer brings together elements of the zeitgeist to be able to speak to their audience effectively.

Section 3 closes with a chapter on how to approach pitching an article and includes samples of two types of letters to get you started.

Finally, we've included an appendix which highlights postgraduate programmes in fashion communication or fashion journalism should you wish to take your studies further.

Fashion writing is more widely recognized now as a serious form of journalism (despite the fact that the first issue of *Vogue* was published in 1892) that goes beyond product descriptions in the Sears *Wish Book* to a discipline that can encompass multiple areas of study or interest. This book endeavours to expand what fashion writing means and give it the attention it deserves as a discrete form of writing.

Nothing Naïve About Fashion

French Fashion Journalist and Editor-in-Chief of Naïfs, *Amanda Winnie Kabuiku, Talks About the Links Between Fashion, History, and Contemporary Social Issues*

From collaborating with publications such as *Le Monde Afrique, Coveteur,* and *i-D Vice France* to being part of the team at *All the Pretty Birds*, Kabuiku has upped the ante with her new publication *Naïfs* and created a space where underrepresented voices and talent are given the credit they are rightfully due.

When did your interest in fashion begin? Did you know you wanted to be a fashion journalist when you were young?

I knew very early on that I would become a journalist. I just didn't have the patterns and the codes. I had an early interest in writing. I was a rather introverted girl. Writing gives me strength. I had a crazy need to express myself. My older sister lived near the BBC, and I visited her regularly. Every time I went to London, I bought *Glamour* magazine. I read the editorials very carefully, and I think the desire to become a fashion journalist came from that. I wanted a place where I needed to talk to people when it was essential to me.

Were there fashion journalists you admired at the start of your career or that you admire today? What is it about their work that drew/draws you to it?

I'm not fascinated by individual journalists. From a general perspective, I like the publication approach more than I like a journalist in particular. I am fascinated by *T Magazine*, *M le Monde*, or *O de l'Obs*. I like this highly documented approach to journalism associated with lighter themes. Of course, I like the direction of *The Cut*, and I like what Lindsay Peoples Wagner did with it. It's accurate, informative, and especially very critical. Imran Amed's *Business of Fashion* is so bold.

Your magazine *Naïfs* was launched in 2021 – in the middle of the global pandemic – and in your introduction to the premiere issue you wrote: "I had this responsibility to find answers to my traumas and all these odd justifications about my non-existence around this table where everything was played out for a long time without you, without me. It was time to build my own table, create a counter-soirée, an alternative space where you all are welcome, of course." Can you talk a bit about your vision for this publication in a world that is slowly coming out of the pandemic?

I think I've always wanted to put out a magazine. The pandemic was there, so I didn't want to go backward. I didn't want a reason, even a single reason to back down. It is also true that I had time to think about it, let things mature, and find a voice that would suit me best. This period was a kind of accelerator because the words of Naïfs came to life before my eyes: the reforms of designer Dries Van Noten, who forgot racial inequalities in his letter to the fashion industry, or the murder of George Floyd by a white policeman. This is quite important because these events have affected fashion a lot. I wanted to make sense of everything and try to place myself on this table where I didn't belong.

What have you found to be the most challenging part of your job? How has launching a publication changed the way you work?

I have changed the way I work a lot. In reality, I have a more global vision, not one that focuses on a well-written piece of paper. I need the writing to resonate with the global focus. It's a radical change for me. I learned to work under a general theme, and it is very challenging for me, because usually, at least for other publications for which I write, I do not have this role of editor. I like that. I think my writing has been impacted, too. I'm more fluid, less didactic, and I don't try to show off. I have regained some pleasure, even though the functions are not the same. Writing is part of my DNA, but I have great pleasure in reading the other contributors and editing, as well.

During the pandemic, designers found themselves looking for alternative ways to show their collections, using film or social media. While we're seeing a return of the runway show, do you think that the prevalence of the use of social media to showcase a collection signals a move away from the more theatrical productions of runway shows which have, over the past decades, been such an integral part of the fashion world and the collection experience? If so, what do you think the impact of that will be?

I may shock you, but I'm not a big fan of digital shows. Clothes need to be on a body, to feel the movements, to move in space. I don't think we can do without that. No machine can replicate Naomi Campbell's walk. However, I remain convinced that, to be more digital, brands must be in sync, but in my opinion, not completely. I like the equal opportunities that digital offers. A small designer can present a collection and have a crazy impact, but in the long term, I do not believe in this strategy, only.

Your work is informed by a commitment to diversity, representation, and accessibility. In the mission statement for Naïfs, you state – "Highlighting the unique facets of previously colonized – and under-represented – styles, we assign credit where credit is due." Has this always been an important part of your work, and how do you find it manifests in your writing?

Of course, I had this need very early on to express myself on this and to highlight people from racial, sexual minorities, etc. I could not do this job without giving a platform to people who look like me. I was fortunate to belong to a more complex-free generation where being Black is a source of pride. I also think that beyond all that, we have to surround ourselves and work with people who care about this as well. I was lucky enough to work for All the Pretty Birds. I was in charge of the Spotlight Designer section, and I was able to put into practice everything I believe in and fight for. *Naïfs* is only an extension of all discussions, articles, and interactions.

What do you believe to be the role, and the responsibility, of fashion writing?

I think fashion tells stories. That beyond the word we tell a story and that a garment is a powerful non-verbal tool. Fashion is a mode of expression, and I think that as a minority, fashion says so many things. I think fashion is political. As a journalist, it is my role to capture hidden messages.

You are a vocal and active supporter of emerging and diverse designers and voices in fashion. What unique perspectives do they bring that more established designers may not?

I think designers today are very political. They have a bold vision and understand the world we live in. I think that is very important. They are indeed using the magic that major brands can offer, but I also think they have that freedom because of their size and independence. Dior cannot approach racism or feminism in the same way. We have to sell and sell a lot. I also think that the different collections per year add to this desire not to dwell on the issues that annoy them. I have a lot of brands in mind that I like with their bold speeches: Pyer Moss, Botter, or Teflar. Can we sell and be political? I think so; it enhances the sense of belonging.

What is one skill that you've found surprisingly important when it comes to fashion writing?

I am convinced that we must have a good sense of observation. We must always keep abreast of current events. I don't think fashion is that important in reality. It's just a reflection of a world, the world we live in. Fashion is a tool, a means, not an end in itself. I also believe that talking about fashion is about the world. Whether it be the war in Ukraine, the rise of diesel, or music, these are all subjects that can be integrated into a fashion article. To try to compartmentalize things is a bit of a stretch. It's a self-reflective loop.

What is the best advice, career-wise, that you've been given? How did it impact your path?

I spoke with Mara Brock Akil [American screenwriter and television producer] on Twitter, and her advice was simple: Watch and sit down to write. Nothing more. I don't think you have to have a crazy pen. The practice does that, and I think you have to jump in and give yourself a chance to try. It's a piece of advice that has changed the way I write. Our job is to tell stories, to open up the discussion.

If you weren't a journalist, what would you be?

Honestly, I never thought about it. I have a degree in economics, and I think I wanted to work for NGOs, like the World Bank or the European Commission, and be a kind of diplomat or adviser in a cabinet. I knew it wasn't my passion, so I quickly got back on track.

Notes

1   Mower, Sarah. "Spring 2004 Ready-to-Wear: Alexander McQueen." *Vogue*, 9 October 2003, www.vogue.com/fashion-shows/spring-2004-ready-to-wear/alexander-mcqueen.
2   Sultana. "A Young Afghan Woman on Breaking Free of the Burqa." *The Economist*, 29 December 2021, www.economist.com/by-invitation/2021/12/29/a-young-afghan-woman-on-breaking-free-of-the-burqa.
3   DiDonato, Jill. "Dressing for the Insurgence: When Fashion Is Far from Frivolous." *Huff-Post*, 9 March 2021, www.huffpost.com/entry/insurgence-fashion-what-it-means_l_60368858c5b6dfb6a735dd9d.

Works Cited

DiDonato, Jill. "Dressing for the Insurgence: When Fashion Is Far from Frivolous." *Huff-Post*, 9 March 2021, www.huffpost.com/entry/insurgence-fashion-what-it-means_l_60368858c5b6dfb6a735dd9d.
Mower, Sarah. "Spring 2004 Ready-to-Wear: Alexander McQueen." *Vogue*, 9 October 2003, www.vogue.com/fashion-shows/spring-2004-ready-to-wear/alexander-mcqueen.
Sultana. "A Young Afghan Woman on Breaking Free of the Burqa." *The Economist*, 29 December 2021, www.economist.com/by-invitation/2021/12/29/a-young-afghan-woman-on-breaking-free-of-the-burqa

Section 1
Foundational Knowledge

Introduction

Just as building a house requires solid knowledge of architecture, engineering, and materials, fashion writing requires foundational knowledge upon which to build a strong and interesting piece of writing. In this section, we start with a little history to make sure you're up to speed. We'll discuss some key figures in fashion through the ages as well as important moments in history that helped create the world of fashion as we know it today. From there, we provide some basic vocabulary to allow you to convincingly write about clothing and fashion in general, and finally, we cover the basics of writing that will help you focus and structure your writing.

1 Where Did You Get That Outfit?

A Brief History of Fashion

As in most disciplines, doing your homework makes you better at it. While we might think of fashion as of-the-moment or *à la mode*, the designs aren't created and conceived of in a vacuum – the historical and cultural context informs it. Therefore, in order to write about fashion with authority, a knowledge of fashion history is paramount. To examine fashion through a cultural context, it's important to consider several cultural factors. The social, political, and economic climate of a time can influence designs and how people wear clothes. Precedence, or historical context, tells us who or what came before that may have influenced a design or designer. Finally, reference serves to inform how a design or designer still resonates or is referenced. It's critical to know who has come before *and* how their designs have impacted the way we see fashion today.

The celebrated *New York Times* fashion photographer Bill Cunningham had a broad knowledge of fashion culled from his years as a milliner as well as a photographer, which he used to make connections between contemporary and historical looks. While working for *Details* magazine, he illustrated the connection between a Giorgio Armani piece and one from the collection of Paul Poiret. He also pointed out that a 1989 Isaac Mizrahi look bore an uncanny resemblance to a 1976 Geoffrey Beane design. While most of us aren't trying to catch designers copying each other or fashion's historical archives, knowing about pivotal and influential designers and collections in the past helps to demonstrate a breadth of knowledge and create a frame of reference to point out the influences in a contemporary designer's work. On the other hand, it will undermine your credibility if you fail to see a connection due to a lack of historical knowledge.

Learning about fashion's history shouldn't be onerous, and thanks to books like Taschen's *Fashion Designers from A to Z* and podcasts such as *Dressed: The History of Fashion* as well as exhibitions at museums and countless documentaries, the past is quite accessible in the present. *Fashion Writing: A Primer* works in conjunction with these resources to help you tie it all together and become a well-versed writer.

We introduced the idea of the zeitgeist – the spirit of the times – in the introduction. The zeitgeist is a kind of cultural mood board that distils the dominating concerns of the day (political, social, economic) down to a defining mood of the period. Fashion is an integral part of the zeitgeist. It not only responds to it through design but is also in an ongoing conversation with it. Fashion contributes

DOI: 10.4324/9781003047629-3

to the prevailing mood of an era, and it also responds to it. Understanding fashion history within the context of the zeitgeist will allow you to make interesting connections and create compelling and informative content.

Fashion exhibitions in museums frequently provide such a context for exhibitions, painting a picture of the social climate that accompanies a trend. Think how the glitzy excess of the '70s spawned punk rock and influenced designers Vivienne Westwood and Alexander McQueen. Likewise, shows also present designers under a shared theme, such as the "Radical Fashion" show at the Victoria and Albert Museum in London, England, in 2001 that brought together 11 contemporary cutting-edge designers including Azzedine Alaïa, Hussein Chalayan, and Rei Kawakubo. Learning about fashion should be a dynamic experience. There's a difference between seeing an image of a Vionnet dress, for example, on a page or screen and seeing it in person. Oftentimes, the perspective can provide essential details about the garment. Seeing an object in person also provides you with information about the materiality and construction as well as a sense of the person who might have worn it. You may be surprised at the difference in the average height of people, for example, which impacts the proportions of the design. A museum fashion exhibit allows you to have an active relationship with the garment.

Fashion does not exist in a bubble. It draws inspiration and influence from what is happening around it. Understanding the times in which different collections are produced helps a fashion writer create a fuller picture of a designer's work and ideally set it in within a greater framework for appreciation.

In the introduction, we introduced the idea of the hemline indicator, a theory that states that hemlines rise or lower depending upon the health of the global economy; however, designers might decide to reflect on the economic landscape through other design choices, thereby embodying that decade's defining characteristics. For example, one cannot see Christian Lacroix's elaborate and sumptuous designs of the '80s without understanding that they are reflective of that era's excesses and embrace of conspicuous consumption.

Conspicuous Consumption

A term coined by Thorstein Veblen in his book *The Theory of the Leisure Class* in 1899, the term "conspicuous consumption" refers to how individuals show off and display their wealth by wearing things others cannot afford.

Social movements from environmentalism to social justice have appeared on the runway through the decades – the slogan tees of Katherine Hamnet in the '80s, Stella McCartney's commitment to sustainable textiles and vegan leather, the US protest/women's march in 2017 exemplified by pussy hats, and Beyoncé's salute to the Black Panthers through the use of their signature black berets at Super Bowl 50 in 2016. You may also see similar designs or ideas across multiple runways during a given season (which are ultimately distilled into the trends for that season). This doesn't mean they're copying each other; it is often that they are individually, but similarly, responding to the zeitgeist. A common consciousness, shared experience, and the creep of globalization mean that more people hear the same message, learn about the same things, and share the same concerns. It's only human that the same influences and messaging show up in different designers' collections, often creating a halo theme for the season.

Technological advances also continue to impact fashion. Fashion, as a distinct business, really grew out of the Industrial Revolution, which we'll talk about more fully in a minute. Technology has allowed designers to experiment with fabrics, surface design, and fabrication methods, as well as with the dissemination of the designs, along with the collection, themselves. Witness the move to streaming shows during the COVID-19 pandemic or the direct-to-consumer online shopping that has helped change the face of fashion retail.

Designing the Designer

While we've all encountered designs that boggle the imagination and have us asking ourselves, "How did they come up with that idea?" designers do not work in a vacuum. They may be reclusive or take off for a remote island to dream up their collections, but they're working within a context and drawing from that for inspiration. The zeitgeist will most certainly be at play here even if they're delving into the archives of a designer from the '20s. Despite this common ground, a designer's own ideas, values, and focus will allow for a myriad of interpretations of and responses to the zeitgeist to walk down the runway. A fashion designer interprets the prevailing mood through their own lens.

In this chapter, we're going to familiarize you with some key designers. This is, in no way, an exhaustive list but simply a selection of those who have influenced and shifted the direction of fashion and are among some of the most influential designers in history.

But first, a little history lesson to set the stage.

While there have always been styles of dress associated with various historical periods (the toga of ancient Rome) or cultures (the dashiki of West Africa), fashion was not a concern of the average individual before the Industrial Revolution. Up until then, unless you were of the aristocracy, you had a small, utilitarian wardrobe that was repeatedly mended and adapted to promote longer garment wear. Clothing was used as an indicator of social status, and when there were only the rich and the poor (a middle class rose in the shadow of the Industrial Revolution), the distinctions were limited to the upper class. Frequently fashions were dictated by the rulers themselves, as with the French king Louis XIV, who indicated who was in favour by whom he allowed to wear red heels (note, heels were worn by both men and women at the time). As Christopher Broward points out in *Fashion*, his comprehensive contribution to the Oxford History of Art series, the court of King Louis XIV (1643–1715) "utilized French fashion as a means of control and self-promotion."[1]

Across the Channel in Britain, the Industrial Revolution, sparked in the mid-1700s, suddenly enabled clothing to be produced at a faster and less expensive rate than before. Cloth up to this point had been made entirely by hand from start (shearing a sheep) to finish (weaving threads entirely handspun). The Industrial Revolution brought with it the cylinder carding machine (Daniel Brown 1748), which brushes the fibres, and the spinning jenny (James Hargreaves 1764), which increased the number of spindles used to spin thread for weaving. Average citizens were now able to purchase clothing for style instead of simply out of necessity. This is a pivotal point in fashion. The zeitgeist contained the appetite for self-expression through clothing for everyone, not just those in high society.

There still weren't individuals considered "designers," as we think of them today. Rather, drapery stores brought skilled craftspeople together to recreate the styles worn by famous actresses and social figures and make them available to the general population. Charles Frederick Worth is often considered the first *named* designer as well as the father of haute couture, and in the following section, we'll see how his success was the result of being in the right place at the right time. The appetite for luxury goods in the Second Empire of France was fertile ground for the birth of the fashion designer as we know it today.

The Designer Emerges: Nine Influential Designers Who Shaped the Fashion Narrative

The Self-Promoting Tailor

Charles Frederick Worth (1825–1895) was born in Bourne, Lincolnshire, England, and began his career as a salesman at Swan and Edgar, a drapery shop in London, which featured textiles and notions one would purchase and then take to a dressmaker to have a gown made. He moved to Paris in 1845 and worked at Maison Gagelin, a premier drapery shop in the city, where his success as a salesman allowed him to set up his own small dressmaking department for the store. He created prize-winning designs on behalf of Maison Gagelin for the *Great Exhibition* in London (1851) and the Exposition Universelle in Paris (1855). These successes paved the way for him to open his own house with partner Gustof Bobergh in 1858.

In addition to his dressmaking skills, it was Worth's talent at self-promotion as well as his association with famous actresses and members of court that also distinguished him and contributed to his rise. It was through Princess Metternich, wife of the Austrian ambassador to France, that Worth won the patronage of Empress Eugénie, the wife of Napoleon III.

Worth's designs were known for their use of lavish fabrics and trimmings as well as his attention to fit. In addition to the one-of-a-kind pieces he created for his special clients, he designed dresses which could be copied for multiple clients as well as distributed outside of France. In this way he also foresaw the advent of ready-to-wear fashions for mass consumption. The House of Worth remained open and under Charles Frederick Worth's guidance (with only a brief closure following the end of the Second Empire) until his death in 1895; upon his death, his sons took control and continued the name until 1952. The house was shuttered in 1956, but in the '60s, the name was sold and the house moved to London. Hylan Booker became one of the first Black couturiers in Europe when he took on the role of head designer at Worth in 1968. The house was again revived in 1999, following another sale, with Giovanni Bedin (formerly of Karl Lagerfeld and Thierry Mugler) as the head designer. The house continues to produce perfumes; however, their final couture show premiered during the FW2013 season.

The Romantic Visionary

Paul Poiret (1879–1944) briefly worked at the House of Worth under Charles' sons Jean-Phillipe and Gaston, and like Worth, was a great promoter of his own image in addition to his fashions. Poiret's designs veered from the restrictive and padded fashions of the times, and he claimed to have set women free from the corset, although other designers at the time, such as Madeleine Vionnet and Mariano Fortuny, were also presenting simpler, loose-fitting gowns. Poiret may have simply been more adept at advertising his contribution, or sexism might have affected the coverage of Vionnet's and Fortuny's designs.

Poiret was known for his interpretation of costume components from what was then referred to as the Orient, which included not only the Far East but also the Middle East. He looked to the loose silhouettes of both the kaftan and the kimono, and his clients responded favourably to his sumptuous designs that featured feathers, pearls, and other ornamentation. Despite offering freedom from the corset, he is also credited with introducing the hobble skirt, which was a tight-bottomed skirt that only allowed women to take small steps, famously saying "I freed the bust, and I shackled the legs." Poiret also created the first known look-book in 1908, which featured illustrations of his designs by the graphic artist Paul Iribe, and he collaborated with famed photographer Edward Steichen, presaging the advent of high fashion photography.

Orientalism

In its most basic definition, orientalism refers to "the styles, artefacts or traits of the peoples and cultures of Asia" (basic Google definition). However, our understanding of the significance of the use of the term "orientalism" has been greatly influenced by the postcolonial scholar Edward Said and his 1978 book entitled *Orientalism*. Said's main argument is that this concept, which was created and defined by imperialist Western ideas, has controlled the way the east and middle east (as opposed to Asia, which is the common assumption) have been understood and characterized, resulting in stereotypes based on colonialist attitudes. Today we no longer refer to the countries or people from the far east or middle east as "oriental" because of the racist and imperialist underpinnings of the term.

In addition to Poiret's commitment to marketing his designs, and himself, he recognized the importance of being part of the elite social circles of the time. He promoted his brand by holding lavish costume parties such as his "Thousand and Second Night" party in 1911. Invitees were told to dress in Persian-inspired dress, or they'd be asked to change into clothes of his design. The party also served as a fashion show as models mingled among the guests wearing Poiret's latest designs.

His commitment to ideas of orientalism and forms of elaborate dress eventually clashed with the burgeoning modernism, and his excessive approach to both fashion and his lifestyle eventually bankrupted him in 1929, leaving him to live out the rest of his life as a painter until his death in 1944. The brand lay dormant until the South Korean fashion and luxury conglomerate Shinsegae International bought it in 2015. Under the artistic vision of Yiqing Yin, Poiret was on the runway in Paris for the FW2018 shows.

The Feminist

The name Coco Chanel (1883–1971) immediately conjures key looks – the boucle suit, the quilted bag, the little black dress – as well as the perfume Chanel No. 5. We can credit Coco Chanel with shifting the way women dressed – from a formal, classic look, to a kind of easy, casual chic. Raised in an orphanage run by the Sisters of the Secret Heart in Aubazine, France (approximately 500 kilometres south of Paris), from the age of 12, it is said that it was there that Chanel learned to sew. Influenced by the clean lines, black and white palette, and common textiles of the habits surrounding her, Chanel brought to her collections the simplicity and effortlessness she had grown up with.

Chanel started as a milliner in 1910 and by 1920 had opened her own design house. She found entry into upper-class circles through her relationship with Étienne Balsan. It was through Balsan that she met the English polo player Arthur "Boy" Capel, who eventually became her lover and muse. Her relationship with Capel gave her access to the parties of high society, which, in turn, provided her with first-hand experience of the kind of wardrobe that lifestyle required. She turned to easy-to-wear fabrics like jersey as well as designs that allowed one to go from the beach to a cocktail party to dinner. It has been said that the little black dress also came out of a perceived need – the need for mourning clothes, particularly for young women, in the aftermath of World War I and the Spanish Flu pandemic.

Chanel closed her fashion house in Paris at the outbreak of World War II in 1939. Declassified documents indicate that she was a Nazi spy, although it is often suggested that she took on this role in order to secure her nephew's release from a German prison; however, Chanel reaped whatever benefits came with that role, enjoying the highlife provided by the Nazi Party. After the war, she moved to Lausanne, Switzerland, into a semi-self-imposed exile. While she was interrogated about her relationship with a German officer after the war, she was not charged as a collaborator by the French government due to the intervention of Winston Churchill with whom she was friendly.

She returned to Paris in 1954, at the age of 71, to reopen her couture house in response to the prevalence of male designers for whom she had disdain, notably Christian Dior, and was met with suspicion by the French press but with accolades by the American and British press. After her death in 1971, the house of Chanel languished as the domain of older women and was seen as a stuffy relic until Karl Lagerfeld took over in 1983 and re-established the brand as relevant and modern through his reinterpretation of her signature looks. Lagerfeld remained at the helm of Chanel until his death in 2019. Virginie Viard, a close associate of Lagerfeld at Chanel, became the creative director.

The Face of New Luxury

Christian Dior (1905–1957), the man and the brand, remains well-known having experienced a revival under the guidance of John Galliano in the '90s. But beyond the contemporary designs and the accessories, Christian Dior was responsible for bringing women from World War II austerity to the bounty of the post-war years with his New Look.

Dior's interest in art and design was evident early on. He started as a modern art gallery owner and mixed with such artists as Jean Cocteau, Salvador Dalí, and the illustrator Christian Bérard. It was Bérard's sketches of Dior's designs that enabled Dior to eventually find work in haute couture.

Dior opened his own house when he was 41 years old, having had to do compulsory wartime duty and then spending time working for other designers, and on February 12, 1947, Dior presented his first collection. The New Look (as it was called by the press), with its nipped-in waists and full skirts, took the fashion world's breath away. The war had required many sacrifices, which included restrictions not only on food but also on fabric – many countries reserved fabric for wartime production, which resulted in women's fashions featuring straight skirts that went to the knee and modest jackets. Dior's designs flaunted the use of fabric in the voluminous skirts that grazed the ankle. The utilitarian fashion of the war years had been replaced by the dramatic styles of the New Look.

Dior died suddenly in 1957. The house remained open and went through a number of different designers until John Galliano became head designer in 1996 and repositioned the label as a contemporary powerhouse. Galliano's tenure ended in 2011 after a video was released that showed him making anti-Semitic remarks. Bill Gayten assumed the interim role of head designer and presented two collections before Raf Simons was appointed artistic director. In 2016, Maria Grazia Chiuri was named the women's artistic director for Dior.

The Youth Culture Whisperer

Mary Quant (b. 1934) shook up fashion in the '60s. In fact, it's hard to think of that decade in fashion without thinking of her. Credited with the introduction of the miniskirt, Quant was actually responding to what she was seeing in the streets. In her autobiography, *Quant by Quant*, she said, "I had always wanted the young to have fashion of their own . . . absolutely 20th century fashion." She serves as the first example here of how youth culture can move fashion forward. Young women were rejecting the staid ways and dictated fashions of the post-war era, epitomized by the New Look, and were sensing the freedoms to be offered by the coming decade.

> ### Youth Subculture
>
> As seen in the popularity of the miniskirt, youth culture has played a role in fashion history. Subcultures form when people differentiate themselves from the dominant culture due to their ideas around politics, culture (e.g. art and music), or sexuality. Subcultures frequently coalesce around music and demonstrate membership through dress, and these subcultures have had some of the greatest influence on fashion. From the '20s flapper, to the mods and rockers of the '60s, to hip-hop in the '70s, each of these moments has been referenced by various designers throughout history. Raymond Williams' theory of dominant (mainstream culture), residual (old ideas that linger from previous eras), and emergent (those that rise in opposition to the dominant) states that eventually the dominant culture will co-opt elements from the emergent, such as the way the hip-hop and skater subculture found its way onto the Louis Vuitton runway. Subcultures are essential for moving culture forward even if they start in obscurity and are viewed with suspicion.

Quant, like Chanel, also started out in millinery, but in 1955, she opened her boutique Bazaar, which became a hub for the burgeoning scene in the Chelsea neighbourhood of London. Her aesthetic was more minimal, and she looked to the fashions of the '20s for their shift dresses and dropped waists when thinking about how she wanted to dress. In addition to the miniskirt, she designed A-line dresses and classic shifts with modern colour-blocked designs and explored the use of PVC and fashion tights (beyond the standard black, brown, and tan) that complimented her designs.

Like Worth and Poiret, Quant was also good at marketing. The windows at her shops were known for their witty and unusual displays (once featuring live goldfish), and her place in the London scene ensured journalists were interested in talking with her. She was also one of the first designers to sign a licensing and distribution deal in 1962 with a major US retailer, JCPenney, which took her designs out of London, across the pond, and into America. In 1966, she was awarded an Order of the British Empire for her contributions to the world of fashion.

In the '70s and '80s, Quant focused on the Japanese market where she sold everything from make-up to Quant-licensed home wear, stationery, and carpets. Her brand still exists today, although she retired in 2000. In 2019, at the age of 85, she collaborated with the Victoria and Albert Museum in London on the exhibition *Mary Quant* chronicling her career.

The Lifestyle Master

Calvin Klein (b. 1942) is another designer who also brought the idea of lifestyle to his eponymous label. Established in 1967, Calvin Klein designs were not only noted for their take on American sportswear but were also largely responsible for bringing casual chic once again to everyday life alongside contemporaries Halston and Perry Ellis. His clothing was streamlined and employed a muted palette of grey, beige, navy, and black. The softly tailored separates were meant to be worn at work as well as at play, suggesting the busy life of the contemporary urban woman.

> ### Annie Hall
>
> *Annie Hall* is a 1977 movie starring Diane Keaton in the titular role. Although the movie is about a neurotic comedian trying to figure out why his relationship with Hall failed, the real star of the film is the costume design. Diane Keaton used both her own clothing and wardrobe provided by Ralph Lauren and ushered in a new androgynous style. She combined menswear elements such as vests, ties, and khaki pants with floppy hats, flowing scarves, and accessories.
>
> > *Earning a Best Actress Oscar and lifetime status as an icon of androgynous style within contemporary dress, Diane's radical sartorial statements set in motion a global trend for the "Annie Hall Look". Consequently, she became emblematic of the 1970s woman who was in the midst of constructing her own strong identity at a time of political revolution – and Annie's symbolic status is one that has held steadfast to this day.*[2]

However, Klein broadened his range in the '70s with jeans, underwear, and accessories (most notably perfume), marketed not only for women but for children and men as well. In the '80s, he courted controversy by featuring a then 15-year-old Brooke Shields in a sexually suggestive CK Jeans ad. He followed this up in 1992 with billboards featuring actor/singer Mark Wahlberg and model Kate Moss in provocative underwear ads.

Calvin Klein stepped down as creative director in 2001, handing the reins over to Francisco Costa, who took the original minimalism of the label and pushed it further into something architectural and modern. Costa stayed with the label until 2016. Raf Simons was appointed chief creative officer but left the company after only two years. At the time of this writing, Calvin Klein was looking for a new creative director.

The Visionary

Rei Kawakubo (b. 1942) and her line Comme des Garçons (French for *like the boys*) took fashion in an entirely different direction. Inherent in her silhouettes is a rejection of the traditional approach to design that is meant to "flatter" and an embrace of the colour black. It was an intellectual response to fashion and the state of the world at large.

> ### '80s Power Dressing
>
> Comme des Garçons and the Japanese avant-garde, which included Yohji Yamamoto and Issey Miyake, came as a direct contrast and alternative to the prevalent style of the era called "power dressing." The late '70s and early '80s saw more women enter the professional workforce. John T. Molloy had written the definitive manual on professional dressing for men, *Dress for Success*, in 1975. In 1980, he followed that up with *Women: Dress for Success*. Basically, the concept was to mimic menswear in an effort to convey professionalism and command respect while minimizing the sexuality of the female body. It could be argued that the Chanel suit, with its knee-length, fitted skirt and collarless, button-up jacket, was the first power suit; however, the '80s version featured jackets with broader, padded shoulders that balanced out the big hair of the decade but kept the knee-length skirt. Initially a feminized men's suit, as the decade continued, more flourishes, such as pussy-bow blouses, ruffles, and brighter colours, were added to the mix. Icons of '80s power dressing were Margaret Thatcher and Princess Diana.

Kawakubo started Comme des Garçons in 1973, but it was in the '80s that her designs first made a global impact. Having previously sold her designs in Tokyo through department stores, she debuted her collection Paris in 1981, showing avant-garde pieces that obscured the body, erased sexuality, and played with ideas of asymmetry and architecture. Her followers were dubbed "the crows" by the Japanese press because of Kawakubo's use of black, and her designs derided as "bag lady" fashion by others, but Comme des Garçons has endured. In addition to her collections, which include menswear as well as fragrances, Kawakubo also collaborated with the Merce Cunningham dance company's performance "Scenario" in 1997. Kawakubo maintains relevancy by not only employing her sharp eye and sensibility but also by bringing designers who share her aesthetic and philosophy, such as Junya Watanabe, Jun Takahashi, and Tao Kurihara, to her stable. In 2017, the Metropolitan Museum of Art in New York City mounted an exhibition entitled *Rei Kawakubo/Comme des Garçons: Art of the In-Between*.

The Hustler

Dapper Dan (b. 1944), whose given name is Daniel Day, came to the fashion world in the '80s via Lexington Avenue and 129th Street in New York City's Harlem neighbourhood. His rise to prominence was intrinsically linked with the burgeoning hip-hop movement, and his early clientele included LL Cool J., Salt-n-Pepa, and The Fat Boys. Dapper Dan saw the pride that wearing high fashion logos, such as Gucci and Louis Vuitton, brought people and used that to create a totally unique style that not only spoke to them but also reflected a distinct preference in dress.

His background was both of the streets – he was a professional craps player as a teen – and the classroom, going back to school through a programme sponsored through the Urban League and Columbia University. It was through this programme that Dapper Dan travelled to Africa, where he encountered the tailors there making African versions of popular Western styles. Upon his return to Harlem, Dapper Dan decided he wanted to be a clothier.

Much of Dapper Dan's material was sourced via "boosters" (shoplifters) he knew who would hit the high fashion names downtown. He had been one himself in his youth. He took the clothing and completely remade it so that the logos were prevalent, creating original designs such as logo-festooned leather jackets with matching leather pants. He also put logos where the original fashion houses didn't or wouldn't, and the price matched the prestige of the logos. If you wanted a Gucci-logoed baseball cap, you would see Dapper Dan. In fact, for many years, Dapper Dan's shop was open seven days a week, 24 hours a day, responding to requests from out-of-town rappers, hustlers, and other players who'd seen photos of his designs. As Dapper Dan says in the documentary *Fresh Dressed*, "I blackinized it. I made it look good on us."[3] His designs have been credited with kickstarting streetwear as a fashion phenomenon.

He kept his shop open until 1992 when a lawsuit by Fendi and then US attorney general Sonia Sotomayor forced him out of business. He continued to work as a designer albeit underground until his career was revitalized in the 2010s. Mainstream success followed in 2017 when Gucci showed a jacket in their Resort Collection that was almost a direct copy of a jacket he'd made in 1989 for Olympic Sprinter Diane Dixon. Dapper Dan partnered with Gucci officially and opened a new atelier, featuring only one logo – Gucci – in Harlem in 2018.

The Collaborator

Carrying the mantel of streetwear forward, James Jebbia, a former child actor who'd previously worked with Shawn Stussy of Stüssy, opened Supreme in 1994 in downtown New York City. Initially created with skaters, downtown scenesters, and artists in mind, Supreme has since moved into a highly profitable global market. Supreme, much like Dapper Dan, noticed kids mixing mainstream brands such as Levi's with luxury brands like Gucci and Louis Vuitton, and the label has made its name through the collaborations with such brands and others.

Supreme is best known for its iconic box logo, which itself is a direct appropriation of the work of American conceptual artist Barbara Kruger. If you were to try to say what the Supreme style was, you might say something vague like "streetwear" or "skater gear"; however, the Supreme logo has been emblazoned on everything from sweatshirts to bolt cutters to bricks to skateboards and more. Much of Supreme's success is based on "drop culture" where brands release a limited amount of product and create heightened demand. The resale value of those products is often many times above the original price, thereby confirming the desirability, and exclusivity, of an item. In November 2020, Supreme was bought by VF Corporation, the same company that owns The North Face, Timberland, and Vans, among other brands. Jebbia will stay with the company, and the brand does not have plans to change its distribution strategy. Exclusive drops of limited-edition goods will continue to be their model.

These nine designers are a mere sampling of some of the artists and creators who have shaped the direction of fashion. With an understanding of foundational history, you should be able to see how they've frequently influenced, or reacted to, each other – whether it was Poiret starting out at the House of Worth (a designer he admired), Chanel returning to Paris after Dior had launched the New Look, or Dapper Dan transforming luxury brand logos into hip-hop fashion. Remember that fashion occurs in a vibrant environment – the world around us. In addition to paying attention to what designers are doing now, pay attention to what's happening in culture, politics, and the world. Finally, do a deep dive into the relationship between designers and culture: are they reinforcing, rebelling against, critiquing culture? Look at how they've decided to evince these ideas. Can you see commonalities with another designer or era? How does this design aesthetic continue and contribute to the conversation with the zeitgeist? Engaging with a curiosity that goes beyond the surface of fashion and interrogating what brings designs forth can transform the way you approach your subject and bring a welcomed depth to your writing.

Fashion Forward

Interview by Abi Slone

Journalist, Fashion Designer, Editor, Television Host, Multi-hyphenate Jeanne Beker Talks About Being One of the First Television Journalists to Cover Fashion

As a trailblazer in fashion media, Canadian Jeanne Beker moved the needle off the charts. When *Fashion Television* first aired in the mid-80s, the founders of YouTube hadn't started second grade, the word "blog" didn't exist, and streaming TV was truly the future. Armed with a cameraman and her microphone, Beker made room for herself at every fashion week runway and backstage where she could bring to life the story of fashion and an industry that was on the brink of blowing up.

For the past 40 years, Beker has been covering fashion, from in front of a camera, as the on-air host of *Fashion Television* from 1985 to 2012, to on the page. Publications include her five books, *FQ: Fashion Quarterly* (which she was the editor-in-chief of), and *The Globe and Mail*.

Who were the journalists when you were at the start of your career that you looked to? What was it about them that drew you to them? Since you pretty much were one of the only journalists covering fashion the way you did, did you model your style after anyone? Or were you truly trailblazing? And what did it feel like to be the vanguard, or did you even realize that you were?

I started out in the world of rock-n-roll and the early days of music television. The show *The New Music* launched in 1979, and the style was really smash-and-grab shooting, really zany reportage. Working on that show was an incredible training ground. Not only for how we shot things and got in there and got the story but for dealing with the egos in rock-n-roll when they were experiencing that medium for the first time. They never had to be on camera before, so all of a sudden we were holding their hands and helping them develop personas to suit that interview style. And that's what happened with designers in the mid-80s [with *Fashion Television*]. Reporting on the designers and fashion had that exact same feeling. A lot of them didn't know how to be on camera, and they weren't necessarily great on camera either. I may have been the first one ever to do a tv interview with Marc Jacobs and Jack Atkins (they were manufacturing his clothes). It was incredible to see what they were like. They didn't understand the medium, but thankfully I understood it and could tell the story.

Fashion Television was really the first of its kind. Elsa Klensch [who was doing fashion journalism from 1958 to 2001 and had a television show on CNN] was more traditional. She cared about the colours and the hemlines, which was stuff we never really got into because we were about the energy and the zeitgeist. We were the first to report on fashion as entertainment, bringing it into living rooms.

Interestingly enough, a lot of backstage was accessible, and designers were very open-minded. Many times we were the only crews backstage. Maybe sometimes we would see Elsa. When you think about it now, it was amazing that we were the only ones.

How was it being a television crew? In a landscape full of print media?

The designers in the fashion world were open to us. But it was other journalists. The print people looked down on television. That was the toughest nut to crack, to get journalists to respect us. *Fashion Television* wanted to capture the fun and the buzz of it all, while newspapers were doing a very serious job of it all, covering the trends and the collections themselves – things that we weren't really covering. I personally felt like a real outsider for a long time.

What did you feel was your role in fashion journalism at the time?

We were really there to celebrate the scene. There were some designers that trusted us, and we were never out to get them. It was never our job to be critical. We were there to tell it like it was but not necessarily to dissect it. I love fashion, but I hadn't studied it. I was simply reporting on a subject area.

How do you feel the landscape of fashion has changed over the past 35 years? Does it make it more challenging to find solid editorial coverage?

26 *Foundational Knowledge*

There is a lot of fashion reportage today; some might say too much. There are too many magazines. Too many collections. It's all much too much and such a blur of noise right now. In this time, for a voice to really be heard, it must have something really special to say. But everything is so readily available now – from video to blogging to social media. And there are so many people wanting to get into fashion. I look back now and think, "Wow! How great that *Fashion Television* created enthusiasm for the scene." Everyone wanted to be part of that world.

It was great that people discovered fashion through that window and that it encouraged people to be themselves, be expressive, be who they wanted to be. Some of the arbiters working today will all say they got their first taste of fashion from our show and they got an appetite.

What has been the biggest change in the fashion media and the industry overall?

The democratization of fashion. The day it all changed for me is the day that Tavi Gevinson [who started the fashion blog called Style Rookie (2008–2011) when she was 12 from her bedroom in the suburbs of Chicago] sat in front of me at a fashion show. Many years later, I realized that I was the one who introduced Tavi to Karl Lagerfeld backstage – this little girl wearing a papier-mâché hat. She was great. Fabulous. Unexpected. A breath of fresh air. Why shouldn't she be reporting from her bedroom? Fashion belonged to everyone. That was the democratization of fashion.

Over the past number of years, fashion coverage has changed so radically. In 1995 I was one of the first ones in the world to be called, at that time, a "cyber host" as the first host of a fashion website. MCI Communications [a large US company, now defunct] came to me and said that they wanted to get more women using the internet, so we created and launched the first fashion website, @Fashion. I used to get frustrated because it would take so long for coverage and information to get out, but it was great pioneering fashion on the internet. It changed so much about how we covered fashion from that point forward.

Where do you think we are with fashion journalism today, with the number of outlets and the amount of coverage from media big and small?

It got out of hand. And what we're seeing now, and have been seeing, is a new reality. The media and general audience is slowly getting rid of what doesn't work or serve the people. I have always wanted to do a museum show about the history of fashion journalism and how it has impacted journalism and the fashion industry. I have everything left, from faxes to invitations to Hermès trinkets and custom Louis Vuitton pouches for media – it boggles the mind. There is no shortage of ephemera.

When did writing for print become part of fashion journalism for you?

My job was crazy because not only was I covering fashion for *Fashion Television*, which had a mandate and was concerned with grabbing celebrities in the front row [when that started happening] and getting sound bites from the designers, but I was also covering the shows and fashion from *The Globe and Mail*. I would write everything down, so I didn't forget anything. At night I would scribble away in notebooks in order to remember the show, the make-up artists, the models – there is so much going on in that world. I would notate everything, and then it would run as a diary. Covering the shows was really an experience on many levels. For me, the clothes were quite secondary. It was the grandiosity, the theatricality of it all – the spirit, energy, and creative drive.

Are there pieces that you wrote, or interviews that you conducted that have stayed with you?

There were so many interviews I can't even remember them all, but there are designers that made such an indelible mark on me as a person, including Alexander McQueen. I did so many interviews with him over the years, saw his pain and sadness and how he differed artistically. It seemed he was injured by the media and tormented by the industry.

Then there was a whole different energy in Marc Jacobs who was, when I met him, a lanky kid with big ideas. Of course, there was Karl Lagerfeld. And Christian Lacroix, what an astoundingly brilliant artist, and how he must have suffered at the hand of big business.

Tom Ford [who was once the designer at Gucci and helped revive the brand] always had a lot to say as did John Galliano [currently the creative director of Maison Margiela], especially during the years when he was designing for Dior [from 1996 to 2011].

I definitely did a lot of wonderful interviews.

Did covering fashion take you into any other aspects of the business, beyond media?

I created my own fashion line, a couple actually. The first one launched just after 9/11 with Eaton's [a now-defunct department store chain in Canada]. People understood that I was a real woman in an unreal world and I was making clothes to make lives easier. I wanted to be able to relate to women up close and personal. We got a ton of press, and it turned out well, and then Eaton's shut down. I then launched another brand with The Bay [another Canadian department store]. This time it wasn't funded by the store and was truly my own line. I think people were receptive. Women who had grown up following me, and so I was a known entity.

If you didn't become a fashion journalist, what do you think you would have done?

Been a photojournalist.

Notes

1   Breward, Christopher. *Fashion*. OUP Oxford, 2003, p. 24.
2   Tindle, Hannah. "Annie Hall's Lesson in Self-Directed Style." *AnOther Magazine*, www.anothermag.com/fashion-beauty/9310/annie-hall-s-lessons-in-self-directed-style
3   *Fresh Dressed*. Directed by Sacha Jenkins, performances by Damon Dash, Alexander Dominguez, and Daymond John, Mass Appeal, 2015 (25:57–26:05).

Works Cited

Breward, Christopher. *Fashion*. OUP Oxford, 2003.
Jenkins, Sacha, et al. *Fresh Dressed*. Samuel Goldwyn Films, 2015.
Keaton, Diane, et al. *Annie Hall*. Metro-Goldwyn-Mayer, Inc., 1977.
Said, Edward W. *Orientalism*. First Vintage Books Edition. Vintage Books, 1979.

Annotated Bibliography

Boucher, François, and Yvonne Deslandres. *A History of Costume in the West*. Thames and Hudson, 1996.
   A broad, illustrated history of costume and fashion from prehistoric times to the late 20th century from a Western perspective. Nearly 1200 illustrations from a wide range of sources accompany this comprehensive survey.

Breward, Christopher. *Fashion*. OUP Oxford, 2003.
   A survey of 150 years of Western fashion and designers, exploring the ways in which our cultural ideals have shaped our fashion and how our fashion has, in turn, shaped ourselves. Topics in this book range from fabric technology to haute couture.

Cumming, Valerie. *Understanding Fashion History*. Batsford, 2021.
   This book discusses the evolution and scope of the academic fashion discipline from the 1600s onwards from a primarily European perspective. This jargon-free text is useful for casual readers, students, and collectors.

Deihl, Nancy. *The Hidden History of American Fashion: Rediscovering 20th-Century Women Designers*. Bloomsbury Academic, 2018.
   An in-depth exploration of early American fashion designers, particularly lesser-known female designers. This book aims to broaden understandings of American fashion history by highlighting the work of comparatively ignored fashion pioneers.

Finnane, Antonia. *Changing Clothes in China: Fashion, History, Nation*. Colombia University Press, 2008.
   A history of dress in China from the late imperial period to the early 21st century. This book challenges representations that position Chinese fashion as unchanging and locked in tradition.

Hill, Daniel Delis. *History of World Costume and Fashion*. Pearson Prentice Hall, 2011.
   An illustrated history of the fashions of Asia, Africa, the Islamic Empire, and the Ancient Americas from the prehistoric period to the present. Including more than 1600 images, this book is useful for designers, costumers, researchers, and collectors.

Laver, James. *Costume and Fashion: A Concise History (World of Art)*. Thames & Hudson, 2020.
   This revised sixth edition explores the forms, materials, motives, and functions of fashion from the prehistoric invention of the needle to the present day. This edition is complete with new illustrations and a final chapter by assistant curator of costume and textiles at the Vitoria and Albert Museum, Amy de la Haye.

McNeil, Peter, and Giorgio Riello, editors. *The Fashion History Reader: Global Perspectives*. Routledge, 2010.
   A comprehensive anthology of theory and object studies on the history of fashion from Western and non-Western perspectives covering periods from the 15th century to the present day. This innovative reader is designed with fashion students in mind.

Moore, Booth, and of Fashion Designers of America, Council of Council. *American Runway: 75 Years of Fashion and the Front Row*. Abrams, Inc., 2018.
: An exploration of the changing modes of Fashion Week throughout its history. This book contains interviews, photographs, and historical overview to contextualize this long-running fashion event.

Mulvey, Kate, and Melissa Richards. *Decades of Beauty: The Changing Image of Women, 1890's to 1990's*. Hamlyn, 1998.
: *Decades of Beauty* is an illustrated history of female fashion from the late Victorian era to the late 20th Century, contextualized with the major sociopolitical events of each decade it covers. Chapters include developments in hairstyling, make-up, accessories, and more for the "in" look for each time period covered.

Palmer, Alexandra, editor. *Fashion: A Canadian Perspective*. University of Toronto Press, 2004.
: This edited collection considers aspects of Canadian identity in terms of fashion over the past three centuries, examining the internal and external influences on the sociocultural domain of fashion. This book contains essays from curators, designers, fashion writers, historians, and other scholars to provide a complex view of Canadian fashion.

Perrot, Phillippe. *Fashioning the Bourgeoisie: A History of Clothing in the Nineteenth Century*. Princeton University Press, 1994.
: A sociological exploration of the rise of ready-made fashion in France. This book examines the ways in which clothing can reflect and instil beliefs, values, and aspirations.

Ross, Robert. *Clothing: A Global History: Or, The Imperialists' New Clothes*. Polity Press, 2008.
: An exploration of Euro-American fashion imperialism that positions the rejection or adoption of Western styles as a political act. This book provides an analysis of the processes that homogenize style and clothing, as well as explanations for those locations in which these processes occur differently or not at all.

Slade, Toby. *Japanese Fashion: A Cultural History*. Berg, 2009.
: A history of Japanese fashion from the late-Edo period to the present day. This book provides theories on how Japan's fashion journey came to be and links current fashion theory to the changing clothing of Japan.

Steele, Valerie. *The Corset: A Cultural History*. Yale University Press, 2001.
: This history positions the corset as a strategy for social status, self-discipline, and sexual empowerment, arguing against the common narrative of the corset as a tool of female oppression. Incorporating research from visual, textual, and materials sources, this book aims to complicate the history of the corset and its relationship to women.

Wallenberg, Louise, and Andrea Kollnitz, editors. *Fashion and Modernism*. Bloomsbury Visual Arts, 2019.
: This edited volume brings together essays from a range of disciplines that examine the relationship between fashion and modernism. Topics span from Italian Futurism to the function of fashion in art.

Welters, Linda, and Abby Lillethun. *Fashion History: A Global View*. Bloomsbury Publishing, 2018.
: A cross-cultural history of fashion that includes a wide variety of non-Western cultural perspectives and explores key issues such as cultural exchange, production and consumption, and the effects of colonialism. This book aims to bring to light those fashion histories that have been neglected by Western fashion studies.

2 It's All in the Details
The Language of Fashion

Bouclé, minaudiere, epaulet – do you know what these terms mean? They're all part of the language of fashion. As with any discipline, there is a specific vocabulary for speaking about fashion, and as a fashion writer, it's important that you know the language. Without a solid familiarity with these and other terms in the fashion lexicon, how are we to be sure that what we're trying to communicate about style, design, and trends is clear to our readers?

The importance of having a clear grasp on the vocabulary used by fashion scholars, writers, editors, and others working in or interested in fashion cannot be overstated. Have you ever read something by a so-called authority in a field and immediately sensed they weren't quite as knowledgeable as advertised? It might be the tone, the way they addressed the subject, or their word choice. The same holds true for the fashion writer. If, on your fashion blog, your description of a garment feels vague and imprecise, your reader will sense that you are unsure of your abilities here. Using specific detailed language will allow you to communicate clearly with your reader and instil greater confidence in your ability as a writer.

Fashion writing, regardless of genre, requires you to organize visual information so your reader has a coherent and accurate visual of what you're trying to describe and to what point.

Start by understanding *what* it is you wish to describe. Are you wanting to highlight a specific garment or the style evoked by a collection? Is the fabric the important message or the silhouette? Remember, when writing about fashion, you are frequently serving as the eyes of the reader.

Since we're just starting out here, let's begin by describing an outfit, which is, essentially, what all collections are built upon. The first thing you'll want to do is identify what kind of garment it is. This goes beyond just "dress" or "pants" to the *kind* or *style* the garment is. If you don't see a description in this dictionary that describes the style, then you'll need to do a little more research. There are many fashion and style dictionaries available, both in print and online, and a little extra time spent searching for the right term will go a long way in creating a visual for your reader.

Next, you'll want to pick the elements to highlight. If you tried to describe a dress from top to bottom, at a certain point, your readers' eyes will glaze over and they'll have lost interest in the item. One can only hold so many details in their

DOI: 10.4324/9781003047629-4

mind's eye, so pick the ones that have the most impact. This might be silhouette, fabric, embellishment, or something else. For example, consider this description of the trends for Spring/Summer 2021 from *Vogue UK*:

> *Away from the underwear-as-outerwear impulse came comfort: wide-leg trousers made for bold strides; floaty, sheer maxi dresses promised easy glamour; and ladylike ensembles pimped with a touch of sportswear felt suitably modern.*[1]

In this example, you can see that the writer has chosen to provide descriptions in broad strokes of select garment styles – wide-leg trousers, floaty maxi dresses, ladylike ensembles – which give the reader a sense of the trends as a whole. Later on, the writer might choose to describe a specific example of the trousers or the dresses, which adds another layer of understanding for the reader. As we'll discuss in Chapter 3, The Write Stuff, understanding the purpose of your piece will help you organize it and choose the most suitable details.

Another element you may want to describe is colour. While you are not expected to have an exhaustive knowledge of colour, familiarizing yourself with the colour wheel "as well as common tones within each hue" will help finesse your writing. Understanding how different values (also known as brightness) are commonly named will go a long way in crafting specific descriptions. In the red family, colours go from baby pink, to candy apple red, to maroon. They're all types of red but vastly different from one another. Pantone has been a major leader in colour cataloguing since 1963 when they introduced a proprietary colour standards system with 500 colours. Since 2000, Pantone has forecast a colour of the year (COTY), which has become an inspiration for not only fashion designers but other creatives as well, such as interior decorators and artists.

Cerulean Blue Monologue

The "cerulean blue" monologue from *The Devil Wears Prada* is a great example of not only the power of description, and the distinctions one can make within the colour blue, but also of how trends trickle down from the runway to the store. This monologue has also been seen as an example of how one can be unaware or dismissive about an industry or group of people from which they think they are exempt from understanding, an argument frequently made in regard to cultural appropriation, which we'll discuss in greater detail in Chapter 7 (www.mic.com/articles/147179/how-in-one-monologue-the-devil-wears-prada-nailed-the-cultural-appropriation-issue).

> *This "stuff?" Oh, ok. I see. You think this has nothing to do with you. You . . . go to your closet and you select out, oh I don't know, that lumpy blue sweater, for instance, because you're trying to tell the world that you take yourself too seriously to care about what you put on your back. But what you don't*

> know is that that sweater is not just blue, it's not turquoise, it's not lapis, it's actually cerulean. You're also blithely unaware of the fact that in 2002, Oscar de la Renta did a collection of cerulean gowns. And then I think it was Yves St Laurent . . . wasn't it? Who showed cerulean military jackets? And then cerulean quickly showed up in the collections of eight different designers. And then it, uh, filtered down through the department stores and then trickled on down into some tragic Casual Corner where you, no doubt, fished it out of some clearance bin. However, that blue represents millions of dollars and countless jobs and it's sort of comical how you think that you've made a choice that exempts you from the fashion industry, when, in fact, you're wearing the sweater that was selected for you by the people in this room . . . from a pile of "stuff."

Ultimately, you want to be able to lift your description from the vague, "the red dress," to something specific and easy to visualize, "the marsala red silk dress with a handkerchief hem." If your reader can see the dress you're describing in their mind's eye, then your word choice has done its job.

Ahead, find a collection of terms to help elevate fashion writing. In this chapter, we are striving to give you a good foundational fashion glossary. This dictionary is in no way exhaustive, but hopefully it will start you on your "fashion as a second language" journey and inspire you to continue expanding your vocabulary.

Terminology is organized by category first and within those categories, alphabetically.

Garments

"Garments" is another term for individual items of clothing – from dresses to underwear to outerwear – but does not include accessories or footwear. This is one of the first identifying characteristics of fashion. Understanding that there are different categories of dresses, for example, will help you build a compelling description for your reader. As you develop your fashion vocabulary, you'll start to be able to move your descriptive powers from a flat two-dimensional suggestion of a garment into a fully realized 3-D vision. While we might conceptualize the act of describing a garment as a layering of details on a form (i.e. the garment itself), it underscores that the garment itself is always a factor. Embellishments, colours, and silhouettes may all come into play, but the garment is the root object.

Anorak

Similar to a parka, this is a hooded jacket designed for cold weather. It is waterproof, shorter than a typical parka, and generally a pullover.

Bandeau

A piece of fabric worn around the bust, to function either as a strapless bra or as a top.

Basque

Derived from the Basque region in Spain and France, this term refers to the extended bodice of a dress or jacket in a V-shape, similar to that of a corset.

Bermuda Shorts

These semi-casual short trousers fall to the knee and can be worn cuffed or uncuffed. The name is derived from Bermuda, the country, where businessmen wear short trousers in the heat.

Bolero

A short, open-fronted jacket without a collar. It has long sleeves and stops before the waist.

Bustier

Similar to a corset, a bustier is designed to accentuate the bust. Once exclusively an undergarment, it is now frequently worn as a top.

Camisole

Shorter than a chemise, a camisole is a loose-fitting sleeveless top typically worn as an undergarment.

Capri Pants

These slim-fitting women's pants that end just below the knee were first created by Emilio Pucci in 1949 and sold in his boutique on the island of Capri.

Chemise

A loose-fitting smock that hangs straight from the shoulders without a defined waist, commonly associated with lingerie.

Cigarette Pant

This trouser is narrow-fitted and tapers to the hem, which is about an inch or two above the ankle.

Corset

A tight-fitting undergarment meant to help shape a woman's body by supporting the bust and constricting the waist; it can also mean a garment worn by both sexes to help support a weak or injured back.

Culottes

Meaning "divided skirt," culottes are a type of women's pants that are cut to resemble a full skirt and generally come to the knee or mid-calf.

Figure 2.1 Culottes.
Source: Courtesy of Ian A. Manley

Duffle Coat

Originally designed by the British military, this box-cut, heavy woollen coat with patch pockets features wooden toggle buttons, which are easier to manipulate in gloves. It is named after a town in Belgium where the fabric was originally sourced.

Gaucho

A loose-fitting trouser that emulates the drape of a skirt, indistinguishable when the wearer is standing but evident as pants as the wearer walks.

Halter

The top or bodice of a sleeveless dress or shirt with straps that tie behind the back of the neck.

Harem Pants

Long, baggy pants, fitted at the ankle, these pants were introduced to Western fashion in 1910 by designer Paul Poiret.

Hobble Skirt

Popularized in the early 1910s when the skirt was often ankle length, this design tapers even narrower below the knees and causes its wearer to hobble.

Jodhpurs

Named after the city in India where they were originally made, these pants are tight-fitting on the lower leg and flared above the knee and were originally intended for equestrians. These are also known as breeches (English riding pants).

Maxi

In fashion, this term refers to a long, ankle-length dress or skirt.

Micromini

A very short skirt (shorter than a mini) that barely covers the buttocks.

Miniskirt

A short skirt with a hemline that is usually at least 10 inches above the knee.

Polo Neck

This term is used in the United Kingdom and South Africa for a close-fitting top with a collar that folds over itself and covers the neck; in the United States and Canada, it is called a turtleneck. It is also called a skivvy or a roll neck.

Tunic

A loose-fitting garment (free of shaping or tailoring) that hangs straight from the shoulders and ends somewhere between the hips and knees; generally worn as a top or short dress.

Turtleneck

See *Polo Neck*. Turtleneck is the American name given to a polo neck. In the United Kingdom, a turtleneck is distinguished from a polo neck by a high collar that does not fold over.

Unitard

Generally made of spandex or Lycra, a unitard is a skin-tight garment that covers the entire body, excluding the hands, feet, and the head. Originally worn by acrobats, gymnasts, and dancers, as a fashion item it is known as a catsuit.

Waistcoat

A sleeveless, upper-body garment cut at waist level with a vertical, button-fastened front opening, worn over a dress shirt and underneath a suit jacket of a three-piece suit. It is also called a vest.

Style

"Style" can be a loaded term and signify different things to different people. There is often a distinction between being fashionable and being stylish, although the two regularly overlap in meaning. As fashion icon Iris Apfel has said, "Fashion you can buy, but style you possess. The key to style is learning who you are, which takes years. There's no how-to road map to style. It's about self-expression and, above all, attitude." When it comes to defining an era in fashion, a type of fashion, or a theme in fashion, it's generally referred to as a style. Activewear, boho, and streetwear are all examples of style in fashion terminology. For our purposes here, we're providing you with some of the style categories frequently referenced.

Activewear

This includes clothing designed to be worn during a workout, such as yoga pants, track/sweat pants, hoodies, and more. As this type of clothing became more acceptable outside of sporting arenas, athleisure became its own category of style. The wearing of leggings outside of the gym, for example, is an example of athleisure wear.

Androgynous

This includes clothing that combines elements of both masculine and feminine dresses or falls outside of traditional ideas of menswear or womenswear, such as skirts for men or boilersuits for women. This is frequently used to avoid gender stereotypes or identification. In recent years, many contemporary fashion designers, such as Telfar Clemens, Rad Hourani, and Loverboy by Charles Jeffrey, have focused on creating gender-fluid clothing.

Boho

A term derived from the word bohemian, this style embodies the loose and flowing looks of the hippie era (maxi skirts, loose tops) and is often associated with festival dressing, such as the Glastonbury and Coachella music festivals where goers can be seen wearing flower headbands and crocheted bralettes.

Business Casual

Sometimes referred to as *smart casual*, business casual is a loosely defined style of office wear, characterized by classic, clean-cut looks, which has taken its cue from business attire but is decidedly more relaxed such as khakis or chinos, polo shirts, blouses, skirts, and low heels.

Formal Wear

This is a traditionally Western category for more formal occasions and often broken into day and evening wear. This includes the distinctions of *black tie* and *white tie*. Black tie is less formal than white tie and usually the dress code for weddings, formal dinners, and school formals such as proms. For women, it includes floor-length dresses and cocktail dresses, while men would be expected to wear either a tuxedo or a formal suit. White tie is also known as "full evening dress," and women are limited to floor-length dresses, while men would wear a classic tailcoat with matching trousers.

Resort Wear

This style of dress is appropriate for resorts or cruises. This is more refined than simple casual wear but not formal or fussy. Many designers added cruise or resort collections to their design schedule to capture the market of smartly dressed vacationers.

Sportswear

Originally used to refer to clothing for active sports, and later to clothing worn to watch sporting events, this term has come to be applied to the broad category of casual wear and is worn at any time of the day and for a wide variety of activities. American fashion designer Claire McCardell (1905–1958) is attributed with the creation of this term. Contemporary American sportswear designers include Michael Kors, Calvin Klein, and Donna Karan.

Streetwear

This style, which originated in the '90s, is made up of comfortable clothing including hoodies, sweats, sneakers, and outwear that takes inspiration from hip-hop, skater, and California surf culture. Brands including Supreme and Stüssy are considered streetwear.

Silhouettes

In its essence, a fashion silhouette is simply a garment's shape or the shape it creates on the body. It can also refer to elements of an article of clothing, such as the sleeve. Silhouettes can be used to emphasize elements of the body, create a unique shape, or be part of an illusion. There are classic silhouettes that are commonly recognized in fashion, like the fit-and-flare silhouette utilized by Dior's New Look, and the construction of garments, and silhouettes that are considered more avant-garde, exemplified by the asymmetry of a Comme de Garçons or Iris Van Herpen piece. As designer Giambattista Valli has said, "The hardest thing in fashion is not to be known for a logo, but to be known for a silhouette."[2]

38 *Foundational Knowledge*

Overall Garment Silhouettes

A-Line

It is a triangle silhouette that starts at the waist or the shoulders and gets wider from the hips to the hemline. First coined by Christian Dior in 1955 in reference to his SS collection, it was then built upon by Yves Saint Laurent's 1958 Trapeze Line.

Bias Cut

Instead of following the straight line of the grain, the bias cut is achieved by cutting on a 45-degree angle (diagonally across the grain). It's used for accentuating lines of the body and creating soft drapes and fluid curves. Madeleine Vionnet is credited with creating the bias cut.

Empire Line

Taking its name from Empress Joséphine de Beauharnais, who was married to Napoleon, the style has neoclassical influences, the bodice is fitted under the bustline, and the remainder of the garment falls loosely fitted over the body. When the hem falls above the knee, it is called a babydoll.

Fishtail

It is a fan-shaped train of an evening gown featured in the mermaid style of dress.

Fit and Flare

This style of dress is form-fitting on the bodice and flares out at the waist, ending at, or just below, the knee. Christian Dior's New Look silhouette is an iconic example of this style although having more fully rounded shoulders. This term also includes the mermaid and trumpet style of gowns.

Figure 2.2 Fit and flare as seen in Dior's New Look.
Source: Courtesy of Ian A. Manley

Princess Line

This is a garment where sections of the costume are cut in one piece, from shoulder to hem, with no waistline seam. Close body fit is achieved by cutting the pieces so that the seams create the shape and by adding darts where necessary. The origin of the style is attributed to Charles Worth, the fashion designer who was influential in Parisian fashion for the better part of the 1800s and made clothing for the empress (princess) Eugenie of France.

Sheath

This is often referring to a dress that fits close to the body and stops at, or just below, the knee – think Audrey Hepburn in *Breakfast at Tiffany's*.

Shift

This basic dress style has simple, straight lines and does not fit close to the body. It was very popular in the '60s and in other periods when unfitted styles were popular, including the '20s.

Tea Length

This dress or gown extends to the end of the shin.

Trapeze Line

Trapeze lines were popularized by Yves Saint Laurent in spring 1958, with his Trapeze Line collection that featured dresses that flared from the fitted shoulder line. The trapeze line reinvented the A-line, what had been "most wanted silhouette in Paris."

X-Line

This is a silhouette with a small waist, emphasis on shoulders, and a full hem that follows in the shape of the letter X. An hourglass X-line is created using belted or fitted waists, padded shoulders, and full skirts and is a popular style for coats.

Hems

Fluted Hem

It is often seen on a pencil skirt where the fabric increases at the hem to create a ruffle-like appearance.

Handkerchief Hem

When the hemline of a dress or a skirt is made up of panels of fabric that fall in points, it is called a handkerchief hem.

Neckline

Cowl Neckline

When a garment has draped, rounded folds around the neckline that falls below the collarbone, it is called a cowl neckline. Emerging as a popular style in the '30s, they are thought to have been inspired by the fashions of Ancient Greece.

Keyhole Neckline

This neckline with a keyhole-shaped cutaway sits just under the collarbone.

Mandarin Collar

This is a small, close-fitting, stand-up collar between 1 and 2 inches high.

Figure 2.3 Mandarin collar.
Source: Courtesy of Ian A. Manley

Peter Pan Collar

Named after the collar worn by Maude Adam in her performance as Peter Pan in 1905, it is shaped to fit the neckline and flat with soft, curved corners.

Sweetheart Neckline

This neckline is literally in the shape of a heart – double-scalloped resembling the top half of a heart. The neckline is designed to accentuate the bosom.

Wing Collar

These are starched collars, that stand up stiffly, with their points folded down to resemble little peak wings – much like a paper aeroplane.

Paper Bag Waistband

Worn both high on the waist, or low slung, a paper bag waistband allows the wearer to cinch the fabric in, gathering the fabric over the belt hooks.

Sleeves

Batwing

Also known as a dolman sleeve, this is a long sleeve, cut wide at the shoulder, tapering to narrow at the wrist to resemble a wing. It has had several eras of popularity, from the Middle Ages to the '40s, '80s, and beyond.

Figure 2.4 Batwing sleeve.
Source: Courtesy of Ian A. Manley

Bell Sleeve

This standard sleeve flares out from the elbow/upper arm to create a bell shape.

Bishop Sleeve

This sleeve is set into the armhole with minimal fullness, and it then widens gradually to the wrist where it is gathered tightly into the cuff.

Cap Sleeves

This short sleeve is cut and seamed to fit on the shoulder and taper to nothing under the arm.

Dolman Sleeve

See *Batwing*.

Puffed Sleeve

This sleeve is gathered at the top and bottom but full in between.

Fabrics

Fabrics (or textiles) are literally the materials of which an item is made, and in today's fashion landscape, it could be anything from duct tape to damask to denim. Understanding the different qualities of these materials is essential. When it comes to writing about fashion, the ability to accurately describe a garment's fabrication can make all the difference. Is a garment constructed with lightweight silk or heavyweight damask? Would the dress hang better if it used denim, or is the feeling of spring brought to life through the use of flowing chiffon? The fabrics used in a collection are just as important as the designs themselves and can make or break a look. As we'll discuss in Chapter 5, the fabric can be the trend of the season. If multiple designers are working with mohair, you'll want to recognize that detail.

Acrylic

A lightweight manmade textile (made from plastic polymers derived from petroleum), acrylic was invented in the '40s and is still in use today. It's often used as a substitute for natural fibres in garments as it is less expensive and less likely to crease or be damaged by wear than other fabrics including cotton or wool.

Bouclé

A type of yarn or fabric with a looped texture created by looping or curling the ply (the layers or strands of yarn). It was popularized by the fashion house Chanel and continues to be associated with their iconic looks including the classic suit.

Brocade

Originating in the 17th century, brocade is a heavy embossed cloth, often containing gold or silver threads. Frequently featuring an elaborate design, it is often reversible and may feature motifs such as flowers, foliage, and scrollwork. Most modern brocades are made with a jacquard loom (see *Jacquard*).

Cable Knit

Yarn knit in a raised loop stripe resembling a twisted cable is called cable knit. Fisherman sweaters, for example, feature multiple types of cable knits to create their iconic look.

Cashmere

This is a type of wool made from the fine undercoat of cashmere or pashmina goats. Prized for its softness and warmth, cashmere also has a distinct drape. It is called *cashmere* after the Kashmir region of India where it is believed to have originated as an industry.

Chiffon

Known for being diaphanous, this lightweight, decorative fabric has often been associated with luxury and elegance. Chiffon can be woven using any number of different fibres – from silk to nylon, rayon to polyester. It is slightly shiny by nature and, due to the fact that it is sheer, is often used as an overlay, along with a foundation garment.

Gingham

Most often seen in lightweight cotton, it's a checked fabric typically combining white with green, red, or blue. It became popular in the United States in the mid- to late-19th century.

Herringbone

A very distinct twill fabric (also referred to as broken twill weave), it is woven in a chevron pattern and is most commonly found in outerwear and suits.

Figure 2.5 Herringbone.
Source: Courtesy of Ian A. Manley

Houndstooth

This is a two-toned pattern of checks and four-pointed shapes. Scottish in origin and originally seen in tweeds, the houndstooth can now be found in many different kinds of fabrications.

Jacquard

This refers both to a type of fabric and the loom used to weave it. As a fabric, it features a raised pattern that is woven directly into the fabric. One of the earliest programmable looms, the jacquard machine was developed by Joseph-Marie Jacquard in 1804. The jacquard machine creates not only jacquard fabrics but also brocades as well as damasks and other such weaves.

Jersey

This stretchy, fine-knitted fabric is often used in figure-hugging garments and is especially good for draping. Chanel popularized jersey, using it in the first designs of the little black dress (LBD). Originally made with wool, jersey can now be found made of cotton, cotton blends, and synthetic fibres.

Lamé

This is a shiny fabric made with either gold or silver metallic threads often used for evening wear or dance and theatrical costumes.

Merino Wool

This is a fine wool made from sheep that is often compared to cashmere. It is used most often in jackets and sweaters, undergarments including long johns, and socks.

Mohair

This is a silk-like fibre, notable for its lustre and sheen, made from the hair of the angora goat and most commonly used in a wool blend to create fabric or yarn. The mohair fibre gives yarn a halo.

Opaque

This is a non-transparent fabric.

Pile

The raised surface or nap of a fabric, it consists of upright loops or strands of yarn. Pile textiles include carpets, corduroy, and velvet.

Plaid

This is a patterned cloth with repeat horizontal and vertical blocks of colour. Scottish tartan is one of the most recognizable plaids. Other common plaids are the Burberry check, gingham, houndstooth, and madras.

Satin

This is a cloth, often woven from silk, which has a lustrous top surface and a dull back. This is frequently used in evening gowns and wedding dresses.

Seersucker

This is most recognizable by the alternating stripes of puckered and smooth fabric. While most commonly woven in cotton, seersucker can be made in various fabrics, from synthetic to silk. The term "seersucker" is taken from the Persian phrase *shir o shakka*, meaning milk and sugar.

Figure 2.6 Seersucker suit.

Source: Courtesy of Ian A. Manley

Shirting

Used primarily in tailoring, this term refers to fabrics that are tightly woven and less sheer, making them appropriate for dress shirts, blouses, or dresses. Common weaves for shirting are oxford, pinpoint, poplin, and twill.

Spandex

This man-made synthetic fabric is popular in sportswear and often used in swimwear, leotards, and hosiery. It can be stretched to 500% repeatedly and not lose its original length.

Suiting

Similar to shirting, this is a general term used to refer to fabrics that are woven for suits.

Tulle

A very fine, lightweight net fabric most commonly made with polyester fibres and used in evening wear and bridal gowns.

Velour

Often confused with velvet, velour is a similar material but has shorter piles, which make it less plush and soft than velvet. Frequently used for casual clothes (in particular track suits) and furnishings, it was made popular in the '70s.

Velvet

This is a clothing and upholstery fabric that is characterized by a short dense pile on one side of the fabric, which is very soft and lustrous. This is frequently made of silk, cotton, or synthetics.

Wool

This is the general term for fibre collected from sheep, goats, and other animals (such as muskoxen); this is valued for its warmth, softness, and fire resistance.

Colour

While developing your familiarity with the various distinctions in colour will take time and practice, understanding some key terms in colour theory can go a long way to aiding you in clear and specific description. As Christian Dior once said, "Black and white might be sufficient. But why deprive yourself of colour?"[3]

Analogous Colours

Analogous colours are any three colours that are next to one another on the colour wheel. They consist of primary, secondary, and tertiary colours and are frequently used to create a harmonious look because the colours share hues. For example, orange is between red and yellow on the colour wheel because it contains both yellow and red.

Complimentary Colours

Complimentary colours are those that are across from one another on the colour wheel. These combinations tend to be bold and create visual vibration. For example, yellow and purple are across from one another on the colour wheel as are red and green.

Hue

In colour theory, hue is synonymous with the term "colour." For example, red, green, and blue are all different hues.

Primary Colour

Primary colours are the source of all other colours; they cannot be created through mixing with other colours. The primary colours – in pigment and fabric – are red, blue, and yellow.

Saturation

This refers to the intensity of the colour. This is different from how light (tint) or dark (shade) a colour is. It is about how weak or intense the colour is and can vary depending upon the environment and the light in which the colour is seen.

Secondary Colour

This is the result of mixing two primary colours together. For example, combining red and blue creates purple, which is a secondary colour.

Shade

When black is added to a colour to create a darker shade, it is called a shade of the colour.

Tertiary Colour

Tertiary colours are those created when a primary colour and a secondary colour or two secondary colours are mixed. For example, when purple (a secondary colour) and orange (another secondary colour) are mixed, they create brown.

Tint

When white is added to a colour to create a lighter shade, it is called a tint of that colour.

Value

This is the term used for the lightness or darkness of the colour or hue; the lighter a colour is, the higher its value. Value is commonly rated on a scale of 10, with pure white a 10 and pure black a 1.

Tailoring Terms and Techniques

The details of constructing a garment and the way it is done can be considered techniques, or tools of the trade. From beading to basting, the ways in which fashions are made are important when describing a garment and understanding what it takes to construct everything from a fast-fashion cardigan to a couture gown.

Saville Row

Saville Row has been considered the home of men's tailoring since the 19th century. Located on a small street in London's West End, royalty, rock stars, and other discerning dressers have come here for made-to-measure suits

> A bespoke suit is entirely handmade from the cutting of the fabric to the sewing, and it takes multiple fittings before the suit is ready. Many of the tailors on the street have a history of crafting military uniforms, which can be seen in the cut and sometimes detail of a jacket. Gieves & Hawkes, which is at number 1 Saville Row, as well as Henry Poole, Huntsman, and Dege & Skinner are some of the oldest shops on the street.
>
> In the '60s, Tommy Nutter took the traditional Saville Row suit and reimagined it with innovative designs and a fresh aesthetic. Three of the four Beatles on the cover of *Abbey Road* were dressed by Nutter (George Harrison opted to wear jeans). In the '90s, Saville Row saw another influx of young tailors, such as Richard James. The street still brings to mind impeccable tailoring and superb craftsmanship.

While not essential, it is beneficial to understand what goes into the construction of a garment. Many techniques are labour-intensive, which is often reflected in the price. Once again, your credibility as a writer will be strengthened if you can demonstrate an understanding of the significance of a detail like 100 hours of hand embroidery.

Appliqué

This is a hand-sewing technique popular in haute and demi-couture; one textile is stitched on top of another to create unique motifs, patterns, or textures.

Armscye

Pronounced *armseye*, it is the fabric edge of the armhole to which a sleeve is sewn.

Basting

These long, loose stitches are used to temporarily secure two or more pieces of fabric together. These are often used instead of pinning when constructing a garment.

Batik

This technique was originally developed in Indonesia and creates patterns by applying wax designs (also known as wax-resist) to fabric and then submerging it in dye. The fabric beneath the wax resists the dye and retains its original colour. This process can be repeated as many times as necessary to create the desired look.

Broderie Anglaise

French for "English embroidery," this technique is a form of "whitework" (white on white) needlework that utilizes features of cutwork, embroidery, and needle lace.

Dart

This tuck is sewn into a garment to shape the fabric for a better body fit. They are found most often in the bustline, the back shoulder, the waistline, and the hipline.

Distressed

This is an area of fabric that has been artificially aged or worn. This is commonly used on denim.

Drape

This refers to the way cloth is arranged on a body or tailor's dummy. This allows makers to work with the way the fabric hangs to achieve a more fluid structure. This is also a term for a type of cut of menswear jacket that capitalizes on the way the garment hangs from the shoulders and waist.

Embroidery

This is a decoration of fabric by using any of a wide variety of hand or machine stitches in the same or a contrasting colour. Different styles of embroidery are often associated with particular geographic regions or ethnic groups. We will see how this distinction can be important when we discuss cultural appropriation in Chapter 7.

Epaulet

Epaulets were originally ornamental shoulder decorations that showed military rank. They have since been adopted in fashion. They can be cut from metal or cloth but are often gold trimmed.

Eyelets

Eyelets are small holes or perforations in fabric. Often used for fastening, they can be set with a metal, cord, or fabric ring. They can be functional, used to pull a cord or lace through for tightening, or purely decorative, as seen in embroidery and eyelet fabric.

Filigree

Found in haute couture, it is a decorative technique, where gold, silver, or copper thread is twisted to create delicate scrolls placed over a fabric's surface.

Gathers

This is a means of distributing fullness in some part of a garment by sewing a loose row of stitches, pulling the thread, and sliding the fabric along the thread to make soft folds in order to decrease the width of the fabric.

50 Foundational Knowledge

Godet

This is a triangular inset (tapered at the waist and wide at the bottom) in a skirt meant to add volume.

Figure 2.7 Godet pleats.
Source: Courtesy of Ian A. Manley

Gore

This is a trapezoidal inset, narrower at the bottom, used to add volume to a skirt.

Gusset

This panel is inserted into a garment to help shape and reinforce points, like the underarms or crotch as seen in tights and pantyhose.

Lapel

These are two triangular pieces of cloth that extend from the collar of a suit jacket.

Ombré

From the French word meaning "shaded," ombré is the blending of colours or tones into one another going from light to dark and frequently within the same colour family. Dégradé is the term for when the colour goes from dark to light.

Overlay

This is often a lace or sheer fabric that has been placed over a different fabric underneath.

Patchwork

This refers to small pieces of fabric sewn together to create a mix of pattern, colour, and texture. Initially a style used to create quilts, the technique can now be seen in clothing design.

Peek-a-Boo

This refers to any part of a garment that has been cut out to reveal skin or underwear.

Peplum

This is a ruffle or flare that extends below the waistline. They are cut either into the bodice or as a separate section attached to the belt.

Figure 2.8 Peplum.

Source: Courtesy of Ian A. Manley

Piping

Often used to reinforce the lines of a garment, piping is edging formed by sewing a thin strip of folded fabric – typically bias binding – into a narrow tube.

Placket

This is an opening in a garment that covers fastenings and gives access to a pocket, or the flap of fabric under such an opening.

Pleat

This is a fold of fabric that is either stitched down or held in place by another construction feature in order to manipulate fullness. Usually a number of pleats are grouped together and may be part of a blouse, skirt, or pants.

Box Pleats

A series of back-to-back knife pleats that form a panel and appear in clusters.

Cartridge Pleats

This is a series of small, rounded pleats most often found in skirts.

Foundational Knowledge

Godet Pleat

This pleat uses triangular fabric inserts in a skirt to provide additional movement to give it more swing.

Kick Pleats

Often found in the back of skirts or coats, these inverted pleats allow more movement and lead up from the bottom hem.

Knife Pleat

Also known as accordion pleats, they are a series of narrow, equal pleats, sharply creased to lie in one direction.

Pocket

Bellow Pocket

This is a large gusseted pocket, often seen on safari/military-inspired garments.

Cargo Pocket

This is a kind of patch pocket, often gusseted for greater capacity, with a closure; this is frequently seen on utility clothing and hunting gear.

Kangaroo Pockets

These are long, lengthwise pockets, often used on hoodies or in sportswear.

Patch Pockets

Sewn onto the outside of a garment, the pockets are made out of pre-cut pieces of material and often have a flap at the top.

Figure 2.9 Bellow pocket versus patch pocket.
Source: Courtesy of Ian A. Manley

Welt Pockets

These are found on the front of a man's tailored jacket, with a handkerchief tucked in to them, or on the reverse of a pair of jeans. They are bound, flat pockets that are finished with a welt or reinforced border along the edge of a piece of fabric.

Quilting

This is a popular technique where two or more layers of fabric are sewn together, often with light padding in between. The fabric created appears padded in appearance and is popular for jackets, coats, and footwear.

Raglan

This is a sleeve construction where the underarm seam of the sleeve is extended to the neckline at the front and the back – said to have originated when a British general in the Crimean War, Lord Raglan, had coats with this sleeve constructed for himself after he lost an arm. This is common in sweater construction.

Ribbing

This knit pattern produces vertical stripes of stockinette stitch alternating with vertical stripes of reverse stockinette stitch.

Ruching

This is a gathered overlay of fabric strips that are pleated, fluted, or gathered together to create a ripple-like effect.

Ruffle

This is a decorative frill of lace or gathered ornamentation of fabric, often used to trim or embellish the wrist or neck. A strip of fabric, when gathered or pleated, will create a frill that adds a ruffled line to a garment's straight edge. Think of the lace ruffles worn by Henry VIII or the Victorians. Today, you'll find them in high fashion and haute couture.

Scalloped Technique

This is a series of convex curves, commonly at the edge of a piece of fabric. Scalloping is popular in haute couture on collars, hems, and necklines.

Shibori

This is a method of ornamenting fabric by stitching and forming gathers in the fabric before it is dyed. After dyeing, the stitching is removed and the crinkled areas are released. The areas protected from the dye by the stitching and gathering absorb the dye in irregular patterns characteristic of these fabrics.

Soutache Braid

This is a flat braid, generally rather narrow. This is applied in rows or, more often, in complex ornamental patterns to decorate areas of a garment.

Spaghetti Strap

This is a very tiny shoulder strap used on garments such as camisoles, cocktail dresses, and evening gowns.

Spangles

These are decorative pieces, usually made from metal or plastic, that have a hole through which they can be sewn to a garment. Sequins, which are usually round and fairly small, and paillettes, which are larger and made in different shapes, are the most common types of spangles. They are often combined with beads in decorating evening dresses, handbags, and other accessories.

Tie Dye

This is a method of dyeing fabric by tying string or elastic bands around preselected areas in order to prevent dye from being absorbed by these areas. The unprotected area takes up the dye, but the tied area does not.

Trompe L'Oeil

Trompe l'oeil is an art technique that has been borrowed by fashion, where a designer creates an optical illusion, through a change in perspective, dimension, or placement. From haute couture to the high street's illusion dresses, this method is a popular way of changing shape or adding layers, belts, and collars. It was first popularized by the designer Elsa Schiaparelli in 1927, when she wove a collar into a sweater.

Tuck

This is a means of manipulating fullness in garments by folding the fabric and sewing a row of stitching parallel to the fold. Fullness is released at the end of the stitching. Tucks and pleats are similar, but tucks are smaller, often being only an inch or less in width.

Vent

In garment terms, this serves a similar purpose to a slit. They are often in the back seam of a jacket, where they have been inserted to let the shape breathe.

Yoke

This is the frame or bar, fitted to a person, or animal, that helps to spread and carry weight evenly. They can also be a frame or pattern that is fitted at the shoulders or the waist, to emphasize the structure of a garment. Bodice yokes were first seen in the 1880s, with the yoke skirt in 1898.

Footwear

Footwear is another essential element of an outfit, and the wrong shoe can undermine an otherwise stunning look. A surprising footwear choice can also, however, offer an opportunity to reframe an outfit, sometimes bringing it into a new environment. For example, pairing a formal, full-length tulle skirt with a pair of simple white tennis shoes can subvert expectations in an interesting way, just as the difference in the heel height of a shoe worn with a pair of shorts can move a look from day to night.

> You can never take too much care over the choice of your shoes. Too many women think that they are unimportant, but the real proof of an elegant woman is what is on her feet.
> – Christian Dior[4]

Footwear design has a language all of its own and understanding not only how to use it but also the origin and history of terms can help contextualize runway and collection looks and design choices. Publications including Fairchild's *Footwear News* are great places to learn more about this industry.

Brogue

This is a style of an oxford shoe (flat-heeled, leather lace-up shoe) with a perforated pattern design on the top. This term comes from the Gaelic word for "shoe" – *bróg*.

Figure 2.10 Brogues.
Source: Courtesy of Ian A. Manley

Chelsea Boots

These are ankle-height slip-on boots with elasticated side panels or side zipper. Designed in the Victorian era, this footwear was an alternative to the fussy button boots common at the time.

Cone Heel

Triangular in shape, the heel starts wide at the sole and tapers narrower, sometimes to a point. They are wider throughout the shaft than a stiletto heel.

D'Orsay Shoe

This term refers to any shoe that has a closed heel and toe but is cut down to the sole at the sides. It can be made with a heel of any type and any style of vamp (front). They are named after the Count d'Orsay (who lived in Paris in the mid-1800s) who is said to have designed them by taking the sides off pumps.

Espadrille

This is a shoe with a canvas upper and rope sole. Originally a slip-on, often with long laces tied around the ankle, currently the term refers to most shoes with canvas uppers and rope soles, flats, or heels. The shoe originated in the Basque and Catalonian regions of Spain and France.

Gladiator Sandal

This is an open-toed sandal with multiple straps running across the foot as well as up the leg, reminiscent of sandals worn by Roman gladiators.

Loafer

The classic slip-on shoe has a distinct slotted strap across the bridge of the foot. If a coin is inserted into the slot, they are referred to as penny loafers.

Mary Jane

A closed-toe shoe, heeled or flat, with a strap across the bridge, they were originally created in 1904 by the Brown Shoe Company. They are named after the comic strip character Mary Jane, sister of Buster Brown, who became a mascot for the Brown Shoe Company.

Mule

This is a shoe of any height, or slipper, usually made with high heel, that has a fitted front, but no back, unlike a sling back that has a strap at the back of shoe. Also sometimes called slides, the distinction between a mule and a slide is that slides typically have an open toe while mules do not.

Oxford

This basic shoe style either laces shut or is closed with some other fastening. Details of styling and cut will vary. Originally, the term was used by shoemakers to distinguish between low-cut shoes and boots. Today the major distinction is in the fact that the shoe has a closing.

Slide

This is a shoe with no back but an open toe. See *mule*.

Stiletto Heels

High and slender, these heels taper to a sharp point on women's shoes and boots. They were named after the stiletto dagger in the '30s.

Wedge Heels

The heel of this shoe is essentially a triangular, unbroken "slice," which runs solidly to the middle or front of the foot. Popular since the '30s, they are often made of cork, wood, or rubber and are sometimes finished in cloth or leather.

Accessories

Accessories can change a look in an instance. Fashion icon Iris Apfel, quoted earlier, is known for her exuberant use of accessories and is an adherent to the "more is more" adage. Accessories are generally chosen to complement or complete an outfit, and their usage changes through time. For example, it used to be that a woman was never seen outside the house without a hat on. Now that hats are not a mandatory element of being "dressed," a hat has become a more notable part of a woman's wardrobe again. Handbags and jewellery are some of the accessory categories that frequently spawn trends. In addition to the items mentioned previously, accessories also include hosiery, shawls, and scarves, belts, and eyewear.

Baguette

This is a small, narrow handbag that resembles the French bread after which it is named.

Cloche

This is a bell-shaped hat invented in 1908 by Caroline Reboux. This hat is one of the most recognizable styles to come out of the '20s and remains popular to this day.

Clutch Bag

This is a small, handheld women's purse.

Fedora

A popular hat shape of the '50s, this is made from a soft felt and distinguished by the centre crease on the head, a pinched front, and snapped brim.

Fishnet

An open-weave, diamond-shaped knit, fishnet is more often associated with hosiery and was a defining feature of punk style. The openness of the weave can vary from garment to garment, which allows for flexibility when it comes to wearing it to the office or on the dance floor.

Hobo Bag

This is a large softly structured bag characterized by its crescent shape and designed to be worn over the shoulder.

Minaudiere

A small evening bag made of metal and ornamented with jewels, worked metal, or other decorative techniques. These bags vary in shape (square, round, oval) and can even be designed to resemble swans, other animals, or buildings like the Eiffel Tower.

Wristlet

This is a small handbag with a bracelet-like strap to be worn around the wrist.

General Terms

Like any lexicon, there is general terminology that individuals use. The following terms don't fit neatly into a category, but they are very much part of the language of fashion.

Capsule Collections

Made popular in the '80s by American designer Donna Karan, the idea was to create a condensed version of a full collection that included just the essentials that don't have to be season dependent, making them much more commercial.

Cruise Collection

Originally catered for a client looking for a wardrobe refresh mid-season for their travels, cruise collections have developed into an opportunity to inject an entirely new, must-have, mid-season collection into the market.

Haute Couture

Nineteenth-century Englishman Charles Frederick Worth is considered as the father of haute couture, and today members are selected by the Chambre Syndicale de la Haute Couture. To qualify, designers much create bespoke garments for private clients. The process must have more than one fitting, and the fashion house must employ at least 15 full-time staff in their atelier, as well as 20 full-time technical workers in one of their workshops. Haute couture houses must also present a collection of no less than 50 original designs to the public every spring/summer and fall/winter season.

Line

Used to refer to the shape of a garment (e.g. clean line), it is also used as a synonym for the collections designers release each season. It can also be used to refer to another label or line a designer has, for example, Marc Jacobs, and his secondary line, Marc by Marc Jacobs.

Look Books

This is a collection of photographs that are compiled by a designer to showcase a collection. They are often used by buyers or press to select garments for editorial shoots or as a wholesale sales tool.

Millinery

This refers to the design, making, and sales of hats and headwear. The term dates to the Middle Ages, when a Milliner referred to someone from Milan.

Pret-a-Porter

From the French, it means ready to wear. Garments sold "off-the-rack" versus made-to-measure or bespoke.

Sartorial

As an adjective, the term relates to a tailor or tailoring, but it can also be used to describe clothing, manners, or a style of dress.

Context Is Everything

Style and Culture Writer Nathalie Atkinson Can See the Change Ahead and Feel the Movements the Industry Is Already Making Towards More Meaningful Fashion Coverage

The Canadian fashion journalism landscape may not be as vast or as deep as some other countries, but the size of the industry has never stopped Nathalie Atkinson, freelance writer and columnist for *The Globe and Mail*, Canada's newspaper of record, from thinking big. Her career spanning two decades has included publication in BBC Culture, CNN Style, *Vulture*, and *Fashion* magazines. As part of the cultural smart set, Atkinson has been a guest lecturer at the Toronto International Film Festival, the Bata Shoe Museum, and the Museum of Fine Arts Boston. Her obsession and commitment to understanding the social history and context of cultural production are present in all of her work, notably her fashion writing.

It's a time of change in every industry, including fashion. How do you feel recent shifts in fashion that have highlighted the imbalances in the industry might impact fashion writing on big and small scales?

I'll say that it feels like all those big designers who welcomed the fashion industry disruption that happened in 2020 . . . it has all gone out the window, and everything's just snapped back to the old structures, which I think are toxic and problematic and not sustainable.

Armani said they were going to go back down to two collections a year, and then capitalism just rears its head again. It's very much what Aja Barber talks about in *Consumed: The Need for Collective Change: Colonialism, Climate Change & Consumerism*. It's things that Andrew [Sardone, editorial director of *The Globe and Mail Style Advisor*] and I, and other people, have been writing for years, but nobody's listening. Let's change the model. The business model is not working. Well, it works for the ten people who own those companies.

It doesn't work for designers.

It's sort of becoming this really interesting, parallel rise and fall of fast fashion, a bottomless appetite that's been fed by us and fed to us by these brands, and the need to feed the internet's appetite for new content. Those things are a perfect storm that feed off each other and have made it so they're creating seven new social posts a day. It's all digital now. It's not about the print product.

I'm terribly cynical, but I feel like there's an opportunity during this time of change in the world, and the industry, to introduce a new kind of fashion writing that isn't service writing and has moved beyond that into cultural criticism and fashion. Like a TV critic or a restaurant critic or fashion critic, or what have you. And it should have been like that all the time. But it's a woman's domain, in theory, so it wasn't.

Fashion writing is an interesting space, especially now. There is material that is very service-oriented, and then there's coverage. Few things capture where culture and fashion overlap or intersect and how fashion is a reflection of where we are societally and culturally. Readers don't necessarily only want to know what they're looking at, but why it looks like that.

Precisely. There is so much beyond that. Like colour palette. The colour mauve, when it was invented in 1856, was an interesting moment which is why for three years everything was mauve because they had the chemical ability to make the colour [thanks to William Perkin] that had previously been only available to the richest people in the world. So you know, there is stuff behind it. It's not just random.

Fashion isn't all you cover, but when did you decide that fashion, in particular, was something that you wanted to write about?

It evolved in a strange way out of the service writing that I was doing because I was a young writer who always had my ear to the ground about a lot of things, including sample sales. This was around the time that *New York Magazine* started to invest more in digital, maybe 2003 or 2004, and *Lucky* magazine had come out, and people in Toronto were really interested in their sample sales. It used to be such protected information, and if you wanted to go to a sample sale, you had to know somebody who knew somebody. I was writing this column for a national newspaper, like a service guide – restaurant reviews and store reviews, and sample sales . . . That's basically how it happened.

When did fashion become part of your beat?

A few years later. The newspaper [I was writing for at the time] allowed me to tailor things to my interests. It wasn't that that Canadian national paper had any kind of fashion critic, and so I was able to make it fairly elastic – the definition of what I wanted to cover. I was always really interested in supply chain and makers and factories and fabricators. It's funny to say the word "maker" now because I don't think that was the word at the time. It was what I was interested in, and I just tailored my work to that.

I would go to New York Fashion Week and go to Paris Fashion Week, but in a really limited way, so I was able to see things high-level, much like an armchair critic. For me, though, it was also augmented with the first-hand knowledge that I was learning like on the ground, sort of autodidactically about sewing and textiles and techniques and fashion history, because I'm always very interested in all social history. So yeah, that's kind of how it came about.

If you were starting to write about fashion in 2003, how does that time frame of expanding the more service-focused aspect of fashion writing meet up, or does it, with the start of bloggers and street style photography?

The thing to look up for that would be something like Scott Schulman [who started The Sartorialist in 2005] and when he came up, shortly before Tommy Ton [who started his Jak and Jil blog in 2005]. But I think the big explosion had something to do with the 2008 economic downturn.

It was all the free publicity. When marketing budgets of these conglomerates contracted, and there was such a shame about ostentation in fashion, the [big] companies were a little abashed and hyper-aware about advertising in such a vulgar way. They understood that they could get all this free coverage from street style. Originally it doesn't start with [the big brands]; it starts with people championing smaller brands, but then, of course, just like with everything, it gets co-opted by capitalism because they can't resist making money.

Now, given where we are with the impact of the COVID-19 pandemic, what do you think has impacted fashion coverage? What is the new? It's almost a post-blogger universe because when they started, they were unique, but it's almost just become one mass of media.

I see this cycle happening in almost every kind of new medium or new form. If you look at the podcasting sphere, which was a way of voices that had been pushed to the margins to carve out a space, now it's just a content farm and one more space people have to participate in, like how brands have to have a TikTok, a presence in all these different mediums.

And I think the same could be said for the phenomenon that was blogging, which largely doesn't exist anymore. Now we have this visually driven microblogging platform of Instagram, which seems to be the dominant way of establishing oneself. I know TikTok is popular, but it is very ephemeral, and so it's not something I'm as familiar with because it doesn't interest me as much. Neither does podcasting, frankly, because I'm very visually driven, and I like the interplay of text and image. I think they're important to go together, especially when you're talking about fashion.

Do you think that social media does fashion coverage justice or that it's just showboating without any substance? Like posting a photo with no commentary? Does it tell me anything as a reader?

I know that different social media platforms all have different functions – Twitter is a town square where you try to be heard, and it has a bit of a more of a tail because people will, in theory, follow a link to a story. Whereas statistically, people do not leave Instagram. You can populate it with a link out and something like 5 per cent of the people will follow that link. So it has to stay native in Instagram for it to work, and I don't follow a lot of fashion accounts. I don't follow fashion criticism that way because I like the fashion history side of things. And I like finding intersections and friction points between different parts of the culture and some fashion writing does that. Like the Pulitzer Prize winner Robin Givhan at *The Washington Post*. I mean, she's been doing that for 20 years. Or Lynn Yaeger's old *Village Voice* column. Lynn's was also really service-y though. It was about where you can buy this, and here's the beautiful thing. For me, the other side of it is, I love beautiful things. I love beautiful clothes. I feel a little impoverished by the fact that it's *all* become cultural criticism. Why can't we have both things [in fashion writing]?

I stopped writing regularly as what you would call a fashion critic in 2014 or 15, and I left the *National Post* and became a contributing columnist for *The Globe and Mail* where the beat I have is fashion at the intersection of culture and whatever else because I was always an arts and culture writer, and I always treated fashion as part and parcel of that in a way that men get to do and women don't often get to do. Men get to be serious sports columnists and news writers and can be interested in food and drinks culture and clothing. And they can write about it as A.A. Gill did for years at the *Times UK*. But when women do it, it is undervalued, especially in a newspaper where fashion coverage has a history of being in the women's pages. So it's either women or gay men. And those are, you know, two groups that are often dismissed by the white patriarchy. I like what I'm seeing in the heritage media fashion coverage and in some of the digital native fashion stuff like Refinery29 when they write longer, and it's text as opposed to just a bunch of photos that we were supplied by the PR, which has been happening since the birth of fashion magazines, influenced by advertisers.

- The first fashion plates and magazines were basically an ad rack for the designers selling their clothes. Advertising and editorial have never been separate. We've had different levels of denial.

- I don't do that kind of writing that strictly anymore, partly because I felt personally conflicted, and I felt it was untenable. I was one of the top columnists at a national paper, and I wrote about books and cultural analysis and television and fashion. I was the Style and Design Editor, and there was a lot of cultural pressure to do these market edits that have a lot of really inexpensive things, always selling something and not in a necessarily thoughtful way. So while I was writing these columns that were more focused on makers and sustainable business models that were equitable for all, I was also sort of feeling like I had to include Joe Fresh or Topshop. After a while, I felt like a house divided against myself, and I couldn't do it anymore.

- As an industry, there has certainly been that move to focus on service-oriented content, so much so that it can become a default setting for even seasoned writers. What are other ways to deliver service in fashion writing that isn't tied to shopping?

- I would get a lot of reader queries because the paper was national and also owned several regional papers, so my work was reprinted in smaller markets across the country, and there would be a lot of questions from readers about how they could identify if something was well made or how to tell if it's good quality and well sewn. And you can't assume that the price tag has anything to do with the quality anymore.

- It was interesting for me to realize that there's a generation of largely women who had parents working outside the home, and they didn't get taught all that home economics stuff. It was a revelation when Martha Stewart would write "How to Fold a Fitted Sheet." In fashion, there's a generation of people that grew up with just service and market coverage, but the writing that's been happening over the past decade has educated people. I've always felt like the education piece was missing because it wasn't something that that a fast fashion generation cared about, for whom that was the main commodity and who wouldn't know what a quality pant was if they tried it on.

Now, the fact that we can start to write these stories that don't have to have a service element and that people understand what we're talking about when we say set-in sleeve and what a twill blend feels like and how it's going to perform, I think is a kind of a win. I used to be told, "Oh, can you not use the jargon, like a raglan sleeve." It's like telling an architecture critic to not use the word "modernism" because it's going to alienate the reader. Well, the reader needs to step up and educate themselves, too.

Who are some of the fashion writers that you either read as you were coming up or discovered throughout your career?

Mary Brooks Pickens who wrote the first fashion dictionary [A *Dictionary of Costume and Fashion*]. I gave one of my copies to someone I was mentoring, so I am now on my second copy of her dictionary. I go into it a fair bit because I still learn things all the time. I loved reading Kennedy Fraser from *The New Yorker*, and I discovered sort of early when I started writing about fashion the contrarian Elizabeth Hawes. She wrote *Fashion Is Spinach* and was a fashion designer and a copyist in the '30s and then became an outspoken contrarian of the fashion system and the whole idea of the mass market.

I always loved reading [fashion journalist and editor] David Livingston, the late, great, curmudgeon friend of mine. After he died, I helped to catalogue and dispose of his extensive library.

More recently, Tanisha C. Ford wrote a book [in 2015] called *Liberated Threads: Black Women, Style, and the Global Politics of Soul (Gender and American Culture)*. It's a kind of scholarly, pop culture, look at civil rights and fashion and the meaning of different things. I read it three or four months before the Beyoncé "Lemonade" Super Bowl Halftime Show, and if I had not read that book, I would have completely missed all the cultural fashion references. As a white woman in Canada, I would not be privy to the southern black experience, and so I always seek out more books like that. What I'm interested in is people doing original research on other things. I have a big fashion library. It's pretty deep. I buy a lot of second-hand things that are out of print, and I buy things that aren't necessarily fashion but that contribute to the cultural and social things I know.

What do you think are some of the things that are fundamental to fashion writing but may be getting lost through the desire to produce content quickly?

This is journalism 101, but you have to fact-check. You have to know enough to fact-check things that are being told to you as facts. People always ask how you become a good fashion journalist, and basically, you just have to be a good journalist and then apply it to that. You do also have to love it. You have to be interested in the material, which I think people often overlook. They think it's all glamour, but, for example, you can't be a restaurant critic if you hate food. Criticism is just four things. It's an informed opinion, thoughtfully expressed.

And the informed piece is so key because also I believe you can't be a restaurant critic if you only like to eat – there are other things about food that don't involve eating. It's the additional interest. It's going that one step further. You don't just like pretty things and to put clothes on. You want to know more about it. You want to be more educated around it.

Do you feel like there's a responsibility for people that cover fashion to seek out the new and interesting up-and-comers?

I do. I feel that way about any journalist on a beat, right? You can't just sit at your desk and wait for press releases because the people who can afford to, or have the time to do press releases, are the people who are already in a relative position of privilege. It's so much more interesting to follow your curiosity. The great pieces in journalism are called "a scoop"; they're not called a press release.

Notes

1 Pithers, Ellie. "The 12 Biggest Spring/Summer Fashion 2021 Trends." *Vogue (UK)*, 19 March 2021, www.vogue.co.uk/fashion/gallery/spring-summer-2021-fashion-trends
2 kidadl.com/articles/silhouettes-quotes-from-movies-books-and-life
3 Hopkins, John. *Fashion Design: The Complete Guide*. Bloomsbury, 2021, p. 79.
4 www.marieclaire.co.uk/fashion/shoe-quotes-the-25-best-of-all-time-61098

Works Cited

Barber, Aja. *Consumed : The Need for Collective Change : Colonialism, Climate Change, & Consumerism*. First Edition. Brazen, 2021.
Ford, Tanisha C. *Liberated Threads: Black Women, Style, and the Global Politics of Soul*. First Edition. The University of North Carolina Press, 2015.
Frankel, David, et al. *The Devil Wears Prada [videorecording]*. Widescreen ed., 20th Century Fox Home Entertainment, 2006.
Hawes, Elizabeth. *Fashion Is Spinach*. Random House, 1938.
Hopkins, John. *Fashion Design: The Complete Guide*. Bloomsbury, 2021.
Picken, Mary Brooks. *A Dictionary of Costume and Fashion: Historic and Modern: With over 950 Illustrations*. Dover Publications, 1999.
Pithers, Ellie. "The 12 Biggest Spring/Summer Fashion 2021 Trends." *Vogue (UK)*, 19 March 2021, www.vogue.co.uk/fashion/gallery/spring-summer-2021-fashion-trends.
"The Kick-ass Shoe Quotes to Live Your Life By." *Marie Claire*, 1 February 2019, www.marieclaire.co.uk/fashion/shoe-quotes-the-25-best-of-all-time-61098.

Annotated Bibliography

Ambrose, Gavin, and Paul Harris. *The Visual Dictionary of Fashion Design*. Bloomsbury Publishing, 2007.

A guide to modern and traditional fashion terminology including more than 250 common fashion terms, concepts, and symbols. This book is complete with illustrations and examples from traditional and contemporary fashion design.

Clark, Judith, and Adam Phillips. *The Concise Dictionary of Dress*. Violette Editions, 2010.
An unconventional dictionary that recasts dress in psychoanalytic terms of desire and anxiety, each entry paired with photographs from reserve collections at Blythe House. Psychoanalyst Adam Phillips and fashion curator Judith Clark here provide multiple unusual definitions for each term.

Cumming, Valerie, Cecil Willett Cunnington, and Phillis Emily Cunnington. *The Dictionary of Fashion History*. Bloomsbury Publishing, 2017.
Updates and supplements the classic *A Dictionary of English Costume* with new terms and revised definitions. This essential revision is useful for fashion historians and students of fashion.

Keiser, Sandra, and Phyllis G. Tortora. *The Fairchild Books Dictionary of Fashion*. Bloomsbury Publishing, 2021.
This illustrated fourth edition contains over 15,000 contemporary fashion industry terms organized into 50 broad categories. This dictionary contains 800 illustrations and is a useful reference for students, librarians, and fashion enthusiasts.

Picken, Mary Brooks. *The Language of Fashion: Dictionary and Digest of Fabric, Sewing and Dress*. Read Books Ltd, 2013.
First published in 1939, this vintage dictionary includes an exhaustive list of fashion terms, synonyms, pronunciation guides, as well as a new introduction on the history of textiles and weaving.

Sterlacci, Francesca, and Joanne Arbuckle. *Historical Dictionary of the Fashion Industry*. Rowman & Littlefield, 2017.
This second edition contains over 1400 dictionary entries on a range of topics from designers to trade unions, as well as an extensive bibliography, chronology, and appendixes. This book highlights the important effects of fashion and clothing on our cultural and social environments.

Tortora, Phyllis G, and Bina Abling. *The Fairchild Encyclopedia of Fashion Accessories*. Fairchild Books, 2003.
This reference provides a broad overview of fashion accessories and their components. A useful book for students and fashion enthusiasts.

3 The Write Stuff
Writing Basics

All writing follows some key rules. This chapter will help you understand some of the broader concepts that will ultimately allow you to craft strong and compelling fashion writing that engages your specific audience.

Writing With Purpose

Any piece of fashion writing starts with a purpose, and this purpose generally falls into one of two categories: to inform or to persuade. Writing to inform may be the most common kind of writing we encounter on a daily basis. It has four primary functions:

- To report new or unfamiliar information (e.g. a runway report)
- To analyse for meaning, patterns, or connections (e.g. a trend report)
- To explain how something works or how to do something (e.g. a service piece)
- To explore questions and problems (e.g. an editorial or opinion piece)

Persuasive writing may more readily register for you as we're frequently lobbied for our allegiance, our money, or our attention. An editorial and an opinion piece are places you often find persuasive writing. For example, you might write an opinion piece on the environmental impact of fast fashion in which you make a case for the reader to care about sustainability in their wardrobes. In a trend report, it might look more like "Ten Reasons to Try the Puffer Jacket." While it doesn't sound like an argument per se, it is already trying to sway your views, which is the purpose of persuasive writing.

Persuasive writing makes use of Aristotle's rhetorical triangle, which refers to the three areas to which a speaker or writer needs to appeal in order to make a convincing argument: logos, pathos, and ethos. Every persuasive piece has elements of each, but depending upon your audience, you may choose to emphasize one of these strategies over the other two.

Logos is most commonly associated with logic, although it originally referred to the content and organization of a piece of writing or speech. When appealing to logic, one should try to evoke a rationale response in their reader through the use of clear reasoning, data and statistics, citations from experts, and other fact-based details.

DOI: 10.4324/9781003047629-5

For example, if you were trying to convince your readers of the importance of sustainability in fashion, you would want to lay out the argument logically and cite statistics about the environmental impact of clothing production. Your argument would also benefit from quotes from designers already incorporating sustainable practices as further evidence of the viability of sustainability initiatives.

Ethos is essentially an appeal based on the expertise of the author. What makes you a credible source? Sometimes readers will infer credibility through the publication outlet or your previous publications. At other times, they will look for you to demonstrate your knowledge through your writing. When you've established yourself as a fashion writer, many will come to associate your writing with trustworthiness. In some ways, your ethos as a writer answers the very basic question of "Why should I believe you?" We'll go into greater detail about establishing your credibility later in this chapter.

Pathos is the one that's often the most popular tactic because it's based on emotion. Strong persuasive writing has a clear pull on the reader's emotion whether that's outrage, sorrow, or joy. Writers should use vivid and concrete language and choose examples that trigger emotional responses.

If we continue with our example of writing about the need for sustainability in fashion, you might highlight the loss of wildlife caused by environmental degradation or the threat posed by polluted waters to families living nearby. While this may sound sensationalist, what you're trying to do is make that affective connection with your readers. Once you understand your audience, you'll also understand which of these three elements warrant the greatest attention.

Know Your Audience

Another common denominator among all writing are the three elements of author, subject, and audience. Even if you're writing in a private journal, these elements are present. The author is you, of course; your subject is a record of your thoughts and activities during that day; and your audience could be your future self, family members, or just someone who finds it in the future.

As the author, it's important to establish your credibility, which we started to touch on with our discussion of ethos and the rhetorical triangle. Even if you are not writing a persuasive piece, you need to establish your integrity as a writer. Starting out, you may not have many publication credits from established outlets. You may also be writing for little to no pay for some of your earliest citations; however, the publication for which you are writing will have a reputation of its own, and readers may already be familiar with it. This applies to *Vogue* magazine as much as it does to the local neighbourhood newspaper. They both will have established a reputation through the subjects they cover, how they cover them, and the writers they hire. You may not always have the luxury of choosing from multiple platforms for publication, but you should always be aware of the reputation of wherever you choose to publish because you will be associated with them once they've published you.

Earlier we mentioned that you can also establish your trustworthiness as an author by demonstrating knowledge of your subject, and knowledge of your audience is also an area you can show that you've done your research. An audience will sense whether an author understands who is reading their piece. We'll give you more insights into how to figure out your audience further on in this chapter.

A good writer should first and foremost have some kind of connection to their subject. This could be anything from a keen interest in it, to an academic background in the subject, to being a professional in the field. More often than not, particularly when you're starting out, an interest is the most we have. What's important is that you show that interest through your writing and the research you do for the piece. If you're not interested in your subject, why should your readers be?

The importance of knowing your audience cannot be overstated. First, you want to grasp what your audience may already know about the subject. Are they professionals in the field or individuals with a broad interest? This helps you decide *how* you communicate with them. You want the reader to feel you know their level of expertise or education on the matter. This plays an essential role in the vocabulary used and whether or not you need to provide background information or definitions.

There are two basic kinds of audiences: simple and multiple. Understanding these two distinctions will go a long way in helping you choose your approach and the language used.

A simple audience is one whose knowledge of and attitude towards (critical in persuasive writing) the subject are easily categorized. Friends and family fall into this group as do professionals in that domain. For example, you might conceptualize your audience for a piece written for *Footwear News* (*FN*) as a simple audience because the publication caters to industry insiders as well as shoe aficionados.

What this means is that you can use technical language without having to define terms. You should be confident your readers will understand. If you were to define common terms in shoemaking, for example, your readers will get the sense that you don't know for whom you are writing. Some readers will be offended and feel patronized, which will not only lose your readers but undermine your credibility as well.

The second kind of audience, the multiple audience, is perhaps the most commonplace. When you have people reading the same article but for potentially different reasons, you have a multiple audience. While we may imagine the readers of consumer (as opposed to trade) fashion magazines as being a homogeneous group, they can be quite diverse. Not only may they come from different cultural or economic backgrounds, but they may have differing levels of education as well. Their reasons for reading an article may range from a passing interest, to a lifelong passion, to a way to pass the time in the doctor's office. With this type of audience, you'll want to create a shared language by defining terms that might not be common knowledge.

Just as we aren't expected to be experts in all areas of our field of interest, we don't always know the readership of a given publication. Fortunately, there are two things you can do to discover this. The easiest thing to do is to become familiar with the publication. Read it. You should immediately get a sense of who they think their audience is or for whom they're writing. These are not always the same thing. A publication may conceive of itself as catering to an upper-middle-class readership of 35- to 50-year-olds, but there will generally be a whole segment that does not fit that definition and who may be reading it aspirationally.

Next, look more closely at the articles published. Can you easily put them into categories? For instance, do they prefer more in-depth coverage, or do they specialize in quick bites of information? Take a look at their fashion spreads as well. What are they communicating via the styling? Does the audience seem to respond to traditional approaches, or are the pictorials more edgy or avant-garde? Finally, consider the language used. What can you glean from the vocabulary and the tone of the writing?

Demographic information is an additional way you can understand a magazine's audience. Not all publication sources provide this, but many do because it is a tool to pull in advertisers. If you can't find a readily available outline of their demographics, see if you can get a media kit, which is frequently given to potential advertisers. For example, the media kit for *Vogue Australia* tells you that the average age of their reader is 38 and their average annual household income is $107,000. If you're still having difficulty getting this kind of information, there are websites, such as Statista.com, that provide readership analytics for numerous international magazines.

From Writer to Reader

You can deepen the way you think of your audience and your writing by understanding the difference between writer-based prose and reader-based prose, as defined and explained by composition theorist Linda S. Flower in *Writer-Based Prose: A Cognitive Basis for Problems in Writing*. These two approaches are distinguished from each other in three areas: purpose, structure, and language.

In writer-based prose, essentially the purpose is to help the writer work out their thoughts and document that process. It most frequently mimics spoken language. The structure confirms this as it does not follow a discernible organization scheme. It often has digressions and reflects the path the writer took to work through their ideas without actively filtering out unnecessary information or highlighting key points. It has the familiar pattern of "I thought of this, which reminded me of that, and then I remembered something else."

In language, it often relies on terms that have either fluctuating meanings (depending on context) or private meanings (the language of "insiders"). Basically all first drafts are written in writer-based prose. It's the way many writers discover and work out what they want to say.

Reader-based prose is what we're striving for in professional writing. Here the purpose is to communicate an idea. We've left the discovery phase behind and now know what we want to share. Structurally, it follows an identifiable organization that reflects either a conceptual or a logical relationship between ideas. It uses a vocabulary of shared terms – words whose meanings are fixed and commonly known, with definitions provided for less common and more specialized terms – and provides transitions between ideas. Reader-based process is first and foremost about communicating clearly.

Digital Fashion Writing: Informative, Persuasive, Expressive

All of the information thus far applies to all kinds of writing whether that be for a print magazine, a website, or a blog. However, writing for online sources has some specific attributes. To start, however, let us distinguish between the three basic kinds of websites. These are informative, persuasive, and expressive. We've already talked a bit about informative and persuasive writing, so you should have a primary understanding of the function of these websites. The original purpose of the World Wide Web was informative. It was designed to enable researchers to share scientific data and research papers quickly and easily. As the internet expanded in scope and reach, many found it a good place to develop interest in specific causes as well as to buy and sell goods and services. Online shopping is an extension of the persuasive aspect of the web.

One of the most popular uses of the internet today is the expressive avenue it provides. The popularity of social media and personal blogs is a prime example of this. Many people have found the web to be a satisfying outlet for expressing themselves and connecting with other like-minded people. Apps like Instagram and TikTok amply illustrate the prevalence of this kind of use.

The following are some ideas for how to structure your writing for web publication. While these are provided primarily for online writing, you may find some of these strategies helpful for print publications as well. Check out the table at the end of this chapter for a quick guide to digital platforms.

Storyboarding is a good alternative to writing an outline for an online piece. A technique most often associated with film and television, storyboarding employs graphics and visuals to organize your work. This allows you to visualize the flow of information and literally use that graphic representation to structure your piece. You can use things like bolded headers to allow readers to access information in the manner best suited to their reading styles and their interests as well as organize it so your main purpose stands out.

Chunking is another common practice in online writing. At its most basic level, this means putting your information into small and easy-to-digest chunks of text. Instagram is a good example of where users naturally do this. One thing many individuals expect from the web is speed, and chunking acknowledges this by keeping information tight and focused. Putting your writing into easy takeaway bites of information demonstrates your knowledge of your audience. You can also employ chunking in conjunction with a more traditional piece of writing by providing a summary of your article in a chunk that serves as a hyperlink to the full-length piece. This allows readers to get a sense of the content of the article before deciding whether to read it or not.

With either of these strategies, you need to think about the sequence, or what we might call organization in a paper-based piece, of information. While many people tend not to read websites in a linear fashion, the information should follow a logical progression. Even if you've decided upon a hypertext-driven piece, each chunk should make sense by itself as well as within the intended order of the sequence.

Style Matters

Many publications – both in print and online – follow style guides. Some will follow more general and established ones such as *The Guardian* style guide, the Modern Language Association's *MLA Style Manual*, or the *Chicago Manual of Style*. However, there may be publication-specific style guides that go beyond grammar and punctuation use to voice and tone guidelines, commonly used words, and even approved fonts. It's always good to find out if your publication follows a specific one. For example, not everyone uses the Oxford (also known as the serial) comma. This is something a writer should know before starting their piece to avoid additional editing down the line.

Understanding the purpose of your piece of writing as well as the intended audience and their qualities will go a long way in helping you compose a strong piece of writing. If we return to the earlier example of your opinion piece on fast fashion, you'll want to research publications that have published stories on sustainability in fashion and get a sense of their focus. Where would your piece fit? What does it add to the conversation? Then take that one step further, and think about how you will communicate this idea digitally. What kind of social media post can you make once the piece is published to connect the print to the digital and vice versa? Your opinion piece will be persuasive, but perhaps your social media post will be expressive. Once you understand how these elements work together to engage a diverse fashion readership, you're well on your way to becoming a fashion writer.

Porter, Please

London-based Writer Charlie Porter Discusses His Accession Into the World of Fashion Writing and What Art Has to Do With It

A degree in philosophy may not be everyone's gateway into the world of fashion, but for journalist Charlie Porter, it was the perfect place to begin. After almost 20 years in the business including stints as the deputy fashion editor at *The Guardian* and the Amsterdam-based magazine *Fantastic Man*, Porter has established himself as an authority on menswear and a bright light as fashion moves into its post-pandemic evolution.

His most recent book, *What Artists Wear*, examines fashion's role in the lives of artists from Andy Warhol to Cindy Sherman, and fashion from his personal collection was included in the Victoria and Albert's first fashion exhibition dedicated to menswear *Fashioning Masculinities: The Art of Menswear* show in London in the spring of 2022.

Table 3.1 Guide to Digital Platforms

Platform	Format and average/optimal length	Tips	Frequency for effectiveness
Blog post	Images and text Trend reports/style guides/service pieces: 150–300 words Editorials: up to 1500 words	• Avoid extraneous information • Adapt length based on focus • Include topical headings • Prioritize images over text	1–4 times a week
Instagram	Images and text Image caption in feed: up to 2200 characters; 125–150 characters (average 25–40 words) suggested for optimal engagement Videos guidelines: **Instagram feed** – 3–60 seconds Image caption information pertains to this as well **Instagram stories** – up to 15 seconds (larger videos cut into 15 second segments) **Reels** – up to 30 seconds **IGTV** – 10 minutes for regular accounts; 60 minutes for large/verified accounts **Live video** – up to 4 hours	• Tone is light and friendly • Quick snippet to interest reader • Script your videos • Use Stories to highlight new Instagram posts or blog content	Average 4–5 times a week, up to daily posts
Substack	Text and audio Email publishing platform; content is delivered via newsletters to subscribers through email; frequently monetized Three ways to create content: 1. Standard text post – no length limitation; however, Gmail will truncate messages that are more than 102KB 2. Discussion thread 3. Podcast/audio	• Create a newsletter that caters to a specific niche • Choose a distinctive URL (Substack URLs are customizable) • Cross-promote newsletter on Twitter and Instagram • Establish regular publishing schedule	At least weekly; optimal 2–3 times a week

(*Continued*)

Table 3.1 (Continued)

Platform	Format and average/optimal length	Tips	Frequency for effectiveness
TikTok	Video Up to 10 minutes; optimal somewhere between 15 and 20 seconds Script: will be more about action than text (average 2.5 words per second)	• Use script to map your storyline and action • Find and define an angle on a current trend • Choose popular sound/music to accompany video • Create problem-solving content like wardrobe hacks	1–4 times a day
Twitter	Image and text Maximum 280 characters; optimal length 100 characters (between 10 and 30 words)	• Up-to-the minute updates • Feature micro-influencers • Host promotions/giveaways • Share fashion tips • Can repost same content but rephrase to make it fresh	1–2 times a day

How did you get started in fashion journalism? Where did you begin?

I educated myself in journalism, through fashion writing and style writing. I grew up in the UK at the time of the *Face* magazine and *i-D* magazine, often spoken about as archetypal, perfect fashion monthly magazines. Looking back now I know they weren't perfect, but at the time, to a 12-year-old kid, they were. That is what I used to teach and educate myself, very knowingly.

It wasn't with a sense of "Oh I'm going to be a fashion journalist," but just in educating myself in counterculture and a way of seeing the world. And to do that I read every single word in the magazine. I looked at everything. From the words in the features, interviews, news stories, even down to the contents page or credits to learn how they used language. So I educated myself in fashion writing. I've never had any education in journalism whatsoever, like formal education. So all of my education was what I gave myself.

What I found in it as a kid was what I find in it now to write about – fashion is this wide-open field. Because it's ridiculed so much people don't really look at it and set the parameters for it, so you can get away with so much. Whereas in art writing or other forms of writing, they're so examined that you can't get away with things, and you actually can say less. And I always found that in fashion writing a piece that looks like it's a bit of fluff can let you talk about politics, economics, society, ecology, oppression, structures . . . you do all the stuff you can do under the surface of something that looks like it's just a picture about clothes.

Nobody's paying attention.

No. And literally, when I worked at *The Guardian*, the farthest you could go at the back of the room before you fell into the book section, which was the farthest, farthest quiet corner where they hid away, was the fashion section, the farthest point away from the central power in terms of where things happened. People would come over to us for a laugh or some gossip or a bit of a chat because obviously we had the best gossip in the office, and we were really funny.

But then also, I was aware whenever any of those people on the features desk wanted to skewer somebody, or when they wanted to pinpoint someone's character or an error in it, the first thing they did was use clothing. So it was a primary tool in writing that everyone used, yet the supposed experts in it were relegated to the back. And that always fascinated me and continues to fascinate me about fashion writing. Also kind of delighted in a way because it means I can continue to get away with stuff because you're "just doing fashion" but actually writing about all these other issues.

When you arrived in the industry, even though perhaps it wasn't what you thought it was going to be, were you pleased to be there?

Oh yeah, totally. What happened was I chose to study philosophy in London. And I very much chose London because of media. It seemed to me that it would be foolish to spend three years outside of London and then come to London and try and find a place within media, so it was a very conscious decision to be in London.

And the course was very lax at that time, which meant that I could spend all my time doing student journalism. I spent two years doing student papers and then, in the way that student papers happen, I completely hated the editor that came in for the third year. I quit and wrote five letters for work experience. I got back four basic printed-off replies with no personality. The one I got an actual handwritten note from was *Vogue* saying, "Come have a chat." They'd had someone drop out and had a work experience space.

I'd written for the student paper about fashion students going to the shows in Paris and trying to sneak into fashion shows, which you could do in the '90s as security wasn't what it is now. So I had some fashion pieces I could show. A couple of weeks after that I was going to *Vogue* when I should have been in college, and I absolutely adored it. I was there for seven or eight weeks and ended up just going between different departments. They let me write small 100-word pieces, but I got my name in *Vogue*. This was '95, so it was pre-internet where there were jobs to do like photocopying the newspapers and handing out the photocopies to the particular editors. I also got to research in the Condé Nast library, which is this incredible archive. I spent a year bumming around Condé Nast after I graduated, but no real openings came up so I got a job on a British tabloid called the *Daily Express*, which now is one of those appalling newspapers and back then, was slightly less appalling. They were looking for a researcher, and in the following few years, I just presumed that I would never write about fashion because I was writing about arts. After all, that's what you did as a young queer kid. But then I started doing some pieces under a pseudonym for *The Face*.

In 2000, a friend was approached by *The Guardian* to be their deputy fashion editor because they like to hire non-fashion people. And she was like, "Why the hell would I do that? But are you interested in this?" So she passed it on to me, and I got the job. It was an unexpected break, but I'd done the work beforehand.

What motivates you as a writer? What do you like about writing?

I find it a satisfying brain exercise. I find it satisfying to get close to something – sort of both paring stuff back and then also building tension. It's satisfying to do stuff with words and sentences.

Do you feel that as a fashion writer that there's a responsibility to offer something other than fluff?

There's that responsibility in all writing. But maybe it just is starker in fashion writing because bad fashion writing is really bad and very empty and kind of hilarious, whereas I think people can get away with bad art writing or bad opinion writing because there's all the posture. Also, because there are so many outlets for mediocre writing, you can go into the writing and subvert it almost without anyone realizing it.

The key thing with fashion writing is that although most people don't do it, there are still ways of subverting it [bringing more than fluff]. You can completely flip the writing and say all this stuff without anyone realizing you're offering depth. They might say [that a piece] is a bit different but not really see what's going on.

When I started it was around the time in London when there was real radicalism – when [Alexander] McQueen was just breaking through, and there was a great newspaper in London called the *Independent*, and *The Guardian* got great rigorous writing. And also in America at the time there was Amy Spindler, who was the fashion critic at the *New York Times*, and she was super rigorous. I think often these things go in cycles so what happened is that things reverted to how it was before when it was just "Oh, that's a nice dress." It can be exciting to be in a time when it's about the nice dress because it means you have room to subvert it. It's also great to come at fashion writing from the outside, to learn about other things, and then come into it with an outside eye, rather than have been educated within it and then have to unlearn that education.

Is there more space in menswear to write about more than fluff? To subvert?

I don't think so. Because there's so little space for menswear, which shows how deep the kind of patriarchal nightmare is in fashion in most newspapers globally. Fashion is seen as the domain of women because *only* women are interested in fashion because that's *all* they are interested in. They're not interested in the serious stuff, which is basically what that means.

The effect of patriarchy is actually that there's less space for men because men aren't meant to bother with it. They just put their suit on and carry on, certainly in

Britain anyway. I think there's equal space, but there just is more womenswear fashion so there is more chance in womenswear to subvert it. Maybe it just seems like a higher mountain to climb because there's a higher mountain of fluff.

Do you feel like we're at a time now where there's an opportunity to insert into fashion journalism things like non-binary and gender fluidity as it relates to fashion? Maybe it's not part of everybody's consciousness, but certainly Harry Styles on the cover of American *Vogue* (December 2020) is a very nice example, as well as the *Fashioning Masculinities: The Art of Menswear* show at the Victoria and Albert Museum in London in the spring of 2022.

Absolutely. But then, as with all conversations around this, there's also a false hope – there is the space within to allow the conversation to happen, but then also there is transphobia among journalists, particularly in this country, in their 50s and 60s, still relatively young humans who are radicalized.

So basically, there are absolutely possibilities and openings to cover what is considered the more subversive elements of menswear. But once you get into it, there are walls being built, new walls being built, which is even more shocking when it comes from someone inside fashion.

Also, a lot of brands say we've designed a collection for a world of gender fluidity, but when it comes down to it, they will be selling womenswear and menswear in a very old-fashioned way to stores that sell womenswear and menswear. And they will be acting in the same old ways. There are always places where there is a lot of talk about stuff but not a whole lot of action.

For individuals who want to start writing about fashion now, what would you tell them?

The biggest advice is to say what you see. It has always been, say what you see . . . Because so few people do. And it's the same everywhere, not just traditional journalism – if you write an Instagram caption, that's writing. The way you craft words is writing. Everything is writing. So say what you see.

Works Cited

Flower, Linda S. "Writer-Based Prose: A Cognitive Basis for Problems in Writing." *College English*, Vol. 41, No. 1. (September 1979), pp. 19–37.

Annotated Bibliography

Clark, Roy Peter. *Writing Tools: 50 Essential Strategies for Every Writer*. Little, Brown Spark, 2008.
This classic writing guidebook is useful for all skill levels. This revised edition is compiled of short essays on writing in fiction and nonfiction.

Lapworth, Katherine. *Writer's Guide to Good Style: A 21st Century Guide to Improving Your Punctuation, Pace, Grammar and Style*. Hachette, 2019.

A general writing style guide that includes the rules of grammar, punctuation, and spelling, as well as information on making writing more readable, accessible, better paced, and appropriate for online audiences. Useful for improving both online and offline writing.

McNeil, Peter, and Sanda Miller. *Fashion Writing and Criticism: History, Theory, Practice.* Bloomsbury Publishing, 2014.

Combining history and theory, this book explores the development of fashion writing and the history of criticism in order to enable students to become better fashion critics. This text explains the tradition of criticism and provides students with the methods and vocabulary to improve their own critical work.

Strunk Jr, William, and Richard De A'Morelli. *The Elements of Style: Classic Edition (2018).* Spectrum Ink, 2018.

This English writing style guide contains the original version of William Strunk's *The Elements of Style* while addressing those grammar rules that have since become obsolete. This book has been and continues to be useful to students and writers today.

Zinsser, William. *On Writing Well: The Classic Guide to Writing Nonfiction.* Collins, 2006.

This 30th anniversary guide contains fundamental writing principles in a clear, accessible style. A suitable book for improving writing skill in any genre.

Section 2
Working It

Introduction

In this section, we get to the three most common types of writing required of fashion journalists: the runway report, the trend report, and the service piece. Each chapter provides specific instruction on how to approach these kinds of writing. We provide details on what to look for, how to interpret what you see, and how to take that knowledge and craft it into a runway review that takes the reader to the front row or speaks convincingly of upcoming trends and how to wear them. Each chapter features an interview with a fashion journalist as well as an annotated bibliography.

4 Ready for Take-off
The Runway Report

Fashion shows have not always been the big, multi-million-dollar, televised, and celebrity-laden affairs that we know now. In the beginning, a fashion show was simply a show of the current fashions, an opportunity to share with select clientele, buyers, and media what the fashion house had for the season. What began at the beginning of the 20th century with English designer Charles Frederick Worth's use of live models instead of mannequins in Paris quickly became Paul Poiret's fancy dress balls and designers' private (for buyers) fashion parades and finally the first fashion week in the United States in 1943.

But it wasn't until 1947 that a designer's collection was photographed for the public, with Christian Dior's debut haute couture collection "New Look" (so named by *Harper's Bazaar* editor-in-chief Carmel Snow) being one of the first collections documented on film. Until then, it had been up to writers and journalists to report on what they saw: they had to attend the show or salon, take notes and sketch key looks, accurately report back to readers, and set trends for the season ahead.

Today, as a general rule, collections are no longer presented in a private studio setting for buyers only. Fashion shows the world over encourage the designers and their team to show the garments on parade – an actual show – that not only highlight the designs and technical fine points of the clothing but also shine a light on the creative vision of the designer and the story they are trying to tell through their collection.

Fashion as Spectacle

Whether it's an all-consuming immersive experience like Chanel F/W2014's supermarket that was driven by the vision of Karl Lagerfeld; the "slim" shows of Hedi Slimane for Dior Homme in the early aughts; the dark funeral-esque farewell show of S/S2014 when Marc Jacobs left Louis Vuitton; Alexander McQueen's "extreme glamour" homage to fashion editor Isabella Blow in La Dame Bleue, S/S2008; or Alessandro Michele's star-studded Love Parade for Gucci S/S 2022 on Hollywood Boulevard, it's about more than the clothes – it's about the experience.

DOI: 10.4324/9781003047629-7

82 Working It

> Pillars of white light strafed the night sky from a vast black stadium erected opposite the Eiffel Tower. Somehow, the Saint Laurent show sensation has morphed into something between an open-air city spectacle, a rock concert, and a brand power rally. In the experiential stakes, public visibility of Saint Laurent under Anthony Vaccarello's creative directorship reaches for miles and miles across the center of Paris; it's an event that gathers hundreds of onlookers, who sit on the walls opposite to see the models passing by. As a phenomenon, it could fuel any number of case studies about how the exclusionary hierarchies of luxury fashion have fallen and dissolved into irrelevance in today's digital world.
>
> Yet for all that, everything that took place on that runway tonight centered around what Yves Saint Laurent did in the 20th century – his Le Smokings and his hippie deluxe Russian collection – and how Vaccarello systematically retools, rechannels, and reiterates it for a new generation. Amid the automated crossbeams of lights swiveling from the floor, he began with reams of micro shorts and Bermuda cutoff jeans; riffs on tailored jackets; Betty Catroux sunglasses; and slick, funnel-leg Western boots.
>
> – Saint Laurent S/S2020, Sarah Mower[1]

And in today's fashion world, the influences, impacts, and considerations on collections call for a more nuanced reportage and review.

This chapter focuses on what is involved in covering a runway show. In addition to providing detailed information on the must-have elements, it outlines the difference between a review and a report, the importance of cultural and historical context, and where to look for inspiration.

The Shows

Similar to our global news cycle, which operates on a never-ending loop of new information, fashion shows have also accelerated in order to meet the demands of the market. What was once a biannual or triannual event, the launch of new collections has become for some designers, non-stop. In a single year, you can now find the following shows in order of appearance on the calendar (based on the Big Four), starting in January.

Fall/Winter

This is one of the most anticipated collections of the season. The Big Four shows happen from February to early March.

Haute Couture

The belle of the proverbial ball, the couture shows are about the craftsmanship, beauty, and pomp of it all. Due to the rules of the Chambre Syndicale de la Haute Couture, the shows can only be held in Paris and generally happen in January and late summer (July).

Resort or Cruise

A relatively recent arrival, resort shows often offer a more commercial take on a designer's style and are aimed at consumers that can't wait for the next fashion cycle. They are generally held in June and July.

Spring/Summer

The other of the two biggest seasons starts in September, and just like the Fall/Winter collection, the Spring/Summer looks will set trends in mass market fashion for years to come.

Pre-Fall

The newest collection season, which shows in December, is released in-store once the spring/summer merchandise has gone on sale but before the fall collections come in. It is a retail, full-price, sales-driven season.

What to Look For

Whether you're looking at a live-stream, walking around stationary models in a salon, or sitting in the front row in the tents, there are things to consider when watching a runway show.

The Guest List

Even before the lights go down, the show has begun. Who is the audience? What is their age demographic? How are they dressed? Who is in the front row? Although the show is not about the attendees, who is there says a fair amount about the collection and the designer. Celebrities can indicate the status of a fashion house, and the celebrity can reinforce the brand's positioning – Rodarte's front row is Tracey Ellis-Ross and Diane Keaton, while Beyoncé and J-Lo grace the front row seats at Versace. But beyond the celebs, there is a lot to observe and learn.

More than the famous folk that bring publicity, important attendees are the buyers (and the media, but we'll get to that momentarily), and although we are no longer in an age where the only opportunity to see the collection is on the runway, how the clothes move, what the general reaction to the collection is, and how well it works with what's happening overall for the season can be best answered by physically attending a show. Buyers are generally the people in the front row who are unfamiliar to anyone not tapped into the industry.

Media, as mentioned, also plays a role in how a writer can assess a show when they're first starting out. Is this show worthy of the industry heavy hitters? Who is representing that major outlet (newspaper, magazine, etc.) in the front row? Is it Anna Wintour (global chief content officer for Condé Nast) or the assistant fashion editor? Shows that tend to get a lot of media attention, like Vetements in

Paris and Proenza Schouler in New York, often have heavy hitters in attendance, which means the label will get coverage, which, in turn, will impact the success of their season.

Key media and industry include the editors and editors-in-chief of major newsstand magazines including *Vogue* (all international versions), *Elle*, and *Harper's Bazaar*; major newspaper journalists; social media influencers; buyers for department stores; and key boutiques around the world and stylists. Outside of celebrities and friends of the designer in attendance, the front rows of any given fashion show are all about the business of fashion.

Other show attendees generally comprise other industry professionals, sponsors, family, and friends, and, depending on the city and available space, the general public. If someone is standing, they're probably a member of the general public.

Looks Are Everything

The environment is another part of the show that precedes the clothing and begins the moment you set foot in the venue. Elaborate sets à la Chanel or subtle detailing à la Balenciaga should be recorded to help set the tone. A runway production is a highly orchestrated affair. Every detail, from lighting, to music, to the models' expressions, and more, is planned. The runway show is often the embodiment of the designer's fantasies and inspiration for the collection. It's the one time everything around an outfit can be controlled (weather notwithstanding) to present it to its greatest advantage, and every care is taken to make sure it communicates the designer's vision. Consider what is suggested by the staging, and see if this is borne out by what happens on the catwalk itself. Sarah Jessica Parker put it well when she said to Marc Jacobs following his F/W2012 show for Louis Vuitton:

> Oh. My. God . . . I'm sure you've already heard it a hundred times and you'll hear it for the rest of your waking hours but that was one of the greatest triumphs, ever. It was cinema, literature, incredibly nostalgic and reminded everybody of a past we don't even know.[2]

A New Kind of Theatre

As you may have already realized with some of the examples of runway shows given, many designers have elevated walking the catwalk into a theatrical production. Following are some shows that have captivated the world of fashion.

- Yves Saint Laurent 1998: Celebrating the 40th anniversary of his career, Saint Laurent presented 300 benchmark looks from his career on the pitch of the Stade de France before the FIFA World Cup final between France and Brazil. The show was seen by 80,000 in-person spectators and 1.7 billion television viewers.

- Alexander McQueen S/S1999: "No. 13" closed with model Shalom Harlow, in a strapless white broderie anglaise dress, being sprayed by robots while being slowly rotated on a platform.
- Thom Browne F/W2009: Thom Browne created an office in the main hall of the Istituto di Scienze Militari Aeronautiche in Florence, Italy, for his menswear collection. Forty identically styled and dressed models sat and work in synchronicity at identical desks as part of the presentation.
- Louis Vuitton F/W2012: Louis Vuitton designer Marc Jacobs recreated a life-size train station, complete with a special one-carriage train pulled by a steam engine, from which the models disembarked to the runway.
- Pyer Moss S/S2016: In the aftermath of the police killings of two Black men (Eric Garner and Michael Brown), Kerby Jean-Raymond screens a short film responding to police racism and violence before his runway show.

What Does It Sound Like

This is a show after all, and with that comes music to set the mood and help tell the designer's story of the season. Take note of what it is playing. How does the music set expectations? Is it fast paced? Does it build suspense? Is it melodic and soothing? Think about the style and the tone. Would you expect couture gowns to come out to EDM? Again, we're talking about what expectations are set in motion even before the first look hits the catwalk.

The First Look

A runway show is a heavily curated and edited affair. How a designer chooses to start (and end) a show is never by chance. This also pertains to the latest wave of designers making short films to show their collections. First impressions are often lasting impressions, and the first look sets the tone for the collection to follow. This is especially true as fashion shows have gotten progressively shorter over the years; designers will work to grab attention and set expectations right away.

Pay attention to whom they choose to wear the first and last looks as this also helps tell the story of the collection. See the section "The Collaborators" to more fully understand the impact of the models on the fashion show.

The Clothes

For the first few rows of attendees (since that is where the buyers and media sit), designers supply a line sheet that is essentially a record of all the looks, in runway order, with all of their elements and fabrication noted. Whether or not it is supplied, a line sheet is key when referencing the collection in the future, whether for a runway report, a broader fashion feature, or a piece on trends of the season. That level of detail will help when contacting the designer for more information. It may seem like taking pictures is the best way to record the show, but in doing so, details can be missed; for example, how a garment moves or small details cannot necessarily be captured in a photograph. There will always be photographs available after the show for media use, so focus on what you won't be able to see later.

While watching the show, be on the lookout for an angle for your report. Is there a theme, like '20s flappers or futuristic androids? Is there a colour story or a print that is repeated throughout? What silhouettes are you seeing? Are the clothes cut close to the body? Are the pant legs wide, narrow, straight, boot-cut, cigarette? Is the sweater tight or oversized? Is it a feminine cut or a more a "masculine-inspired" look? What fabrics and textures are highlighted? Is it wool tweed or silk, vegan leather or neoprene? Detailed notes on the key looks are essential in writing a runway report.

Most runway reports are filed shortly after the show, but if time is available, the best way to be able to speak to tailoring, finishing, and feel as a new fashion writer is to ask for a studio visit and actually touch the clothes. Most small labels will welcome the interest and coverage.

Context

Nothing creative is ever created in a vacuum. Outside influences affect everything from art to literature to music and film, and fashion is no different, where the world politically (elections, environment, economics, etc.) or culturally impacts each and every collection. It may be manifest in the choice of fabric (less environmental impact), the cut of the shirt (lean times call for leaner looks), or the colourways. Sometimes it's overt like the late-'80s designs of British designer Katherine Hamnett whose oversized T-shirts sported bold polemic statements; sometimes it's implied like the pop culture stylings of American designer Jeremy Scott, who has referenced McDonald's and SpongeBob SquarePants in his designs. Be aware of the world outside you while taking in the world of the designer's imagination.

> [I]n Katrantzou's time, her line reaches . . . internationally based clientele, some of whom collect her work, season by season as souvenirs of her themes, almost as they also buy works of art. Strangely, then, the most extravagant pieces in this collection can be judged as her most commercial – such as the intensely beaded, multicolored dresses smothered in swirlingly collaged motifs of flowers and vegetation. In an era where mass production makes less and less sense for either designers or for wealthy consumers seeking rarity, this is increasingly the way planet fashion is spinning.
>
> – F/W2019, Sarah Mower[3]

Past, Present, and Future

Understanding not only a designer's fashion history but also a bit of history about contemporary fashion shows can better help hone reviewing skills as well as give a foundation to reportage. Before attending a show, try to have a clear idea of what the designer or brand is known for as well as the reception their collections have received in the past. You may want to watch a few interviews with the designer beforehand to see if they offer additional insight.

There are designers who have, over the past 15 years, made a significant impact on how we expect to see fashion shows and how fashion shows are thusly presented. Marc Jacobs for Louis Vuitton, Alexander McQueen, John Galliano for Christian Dior and now Maison Margiela, Karl Lagerfeld at Chanel, and Rei Kawakubo for Comme des Garçons have all changed the face of fashion shows.

Unless it is a designer's first collection ever, there is always something to build on, a collection to provide context for the current collection, and a look to the future. And even with a first collection, a designer will reveal their inspiration in their garments if you look hard enough.

Prêt-à-Porter

Robert Altman's 1994 film *Prêt-à-Porter* (retitled *Ready to Wear* for the US market) was the first time a celebrated filmmaker, known as an auteur rather than a mainstream Hollywood director, turned their attention to the fashion world. Known for films such as *M*A*S*H*, *Nashville*, *The Player*, and *Gosford Park*, Altman's filmic imagining of the fashion world surprised many. The satirical film takes place during Paris Fashion Week and features an ensemble cast that included Forest Whitaker, Tracey Ullman, Sophia Loren, Julia Roberts, and Tim Robbins as well as cameos by famous designers and models. The National Board of Review (a New York-based non-profit organization made up of film lovers, filmmakers, industry professionals, and academics) presented the case the award for Best Acting Ensemble.

While not a critical success, the film captures the interplay of fashion journalists, designers, models, and others in the fashion business from the lens of someone outside the industry. As Altman himself said when asked why he was interested in making this film, "I don't know ... about the fashion business, and that's why it fascinated me. All the politics and backbiting and internecine warfare – it's like espionage was 20 or 30 years ago, but better dressed." It has been said that the streaming service Paramount+ was considering a series based on the film.

The Collaborators

A show is never simply the designer. There are many people involved making sure the show is successful, and there are certain roles on the team that impact greatly how the collection is seen and received. Understanding the function of these individuals can add depth and nuance to your report.

Models

The women and men who walk the shows are more than vehicles for the clothes, and their role is not to be overlooked. Some models have walked without pay for designers they especially like or are friends with. Sometimes it's about branding. A model may be synonymous with the design house, like Cara Delevigne was for many years with Burberry, or the same model may appear in almost every single one of a designer's runway shows like Karen Elson walking for American designer Anna Sui.

As far as what model choices can say about a collection, take, for example, the Saint Laurent review earlier in this chapter from Mower. It is clear how the choice of models plays into what Vacarello is trying to communicate with the collection. By having "the supers" (in this case, Stella Tennant and Naomi Campbell) start and finish the formal tuxedo wear, the message was clearly about classics, no matter the generation. Using an up-and-comer like Kaia Jordan Gerber or Gigi Hadid would not have telegraphed the same message.

Makeup Artists

Beauty trends are also made on the runways of the world, and the people behind the beauty looks not only have influence outside of fashion but also are chosen for their talents for telling a story. Makeup and hair are carefully designed to enhance the designer's conceptual vision for the collection; for example, Pat McGrath's colour blocking lip look at Christian Dior Fall Couture 2012 reinforced the statement-making collection by holding up to the bold prints and colours of the clothing itself. There are many who have been influential over the years, but there are a handful who are widely recognized and dominate. Many of the beauty trends we have in any given season are thanks to the runway looks from McGrath, Gucci Westman, Tom Pecheux, and Dick Page.

Stylists

More than someone who can put together a look for a magazine editorial or a stroll down a red carpet, stylists play a large role in how clothes look coming down the runway – who they are on, what they are paired with, and in what order they walk. Carlyne Cerf de Dudzeele is an example of a stylist who has almost as much influence and vision as the designers themselves but works behind the scenes. It was de Dudzeele who first championed street style by putting model Michaela Bercu on the cover of *Vogue* in 1988 wearing a Christian Lacroix jacket with jeans.

The Reporters

In the world of fashion reporting and criticism, there are the standouts – Suzy Menkes, Cathy Horyn, Sarah Mower, Tim Blanks, and Robin Givhan, among a select few others. Their styles are different, but their goal is the same – to tell the story.

Developing a personal writing style, while remaining true to the fashion and learning about the history and context, gives a report or review substance and authority that enhances the reader's experience and demonstrates your expertise.

For example, consider these excerpts from reviews of the S/S2019 Tom Ford show by Tim Blanks and Suzy Menkes. In the first one, Blanks seems to stand outside his review, almost like an omniscient narrator, whereas Menkes is boldly a character within hers. These very different approaches highlight the distinctive voices of the journalists while still creating a vivid picture for the reader.

From "At Tom Ford, Echoes of Collections Past," by Tim Blanks:[4]

> *The music was a veritable story in song, seductive in its narrative groove. More so, unfortunately, than the clothes, where the narrative was more rut than groove.*
>
> *Hard and soft, restraint and release . . . these dialogues are old friends in Ford's fashion. Here, the strictness of a velvet corset hemmed in the loucheness of a portrait-necklined dress in fluid georgette. Joan Smalls walked in a fitted leopard jacket and bustier that topped a cascade of shivering silk threads. Mock croc made a black lacquered carapace for lace-trimmed lingerie looks. It's an odd sensation when such effortlessly sensual clothes leave you cold. Could have been the colour palette, shades of mushroom and pale lilac and the colour that paint charts call "dead salmon" (there were definite echoes of Ford's colour scheme for YSL).*

From "#SuzyNYFW: Tom Ford – Seducing Clients As Much As The Camera," by Suzy Menkes:[5]

> *I stroked a leather jacket embossed to give the effect of crocodile and slid my fingers over the different depths of black. All around me – holding up dresses with inserts of silk and animal patterns; examining lean, body-conscious dresses; and trying on the dangerously pointed shoes, were potential clients – some of the 132 members of the audience who had watched the show, along with a raft of movie stars, at the Park Avenue Armory in Manhattan.*
>
> *Alas, trapped on my plane from London, running six hours late, I was not one of them. But my visit the following morning to the Tom Ford store on Madison Avenue, where the collection was touchable and viewable up close, may have taught me more about what Tom was trying to say. Gone were last season's garish colours, stretch leggings, and Hollywood glam. Maybe, if I had been sitting near Tom Hanks at the show, I would have felt a frisson of the Ford star power. But the designer has slipped away from non-stop paparazzi-friendly fashion. And he said so.*

Putting Pen to Paper

Once you've seen the collection and taken all the notes, it's time to organize your thoughts and write the report. You'll be sifting through a lot of information, and now is the time to figure how you want to organize that. It might be around key looks or a specific theme. A runway report is not simply a listing of looks; it's basically the story you've brought back from the show. Good reportage often has a narrative arc.

Regardless of a writer's personal style, there are fundamental elements that should appear in every report. They include the season, the designer, and the name of the show. Remember that this is a form of journalism, and answering who, what, when, where, and how (this would be the specifics of the looks) are details a reader will expect.

As discussed earlier, fabrication, key looks, how a garment moves, the colour story, and environmental notes (like lighting and music) should all be included as those elements help to tell the designer's story for the season. One of these could be the angle around which you structure your report.

The use of fashion-specific language to describe shapes, cuts, and tailoring is essential, as is developing a nuanced colour vocabulary. You can't describe every look, so pick the ones that are exemplars of the collection. A reader should get a sense of the collection as a whole. References to other collections of the same designer can further provide context and authority to the report.

Think about how you open your report. Are you a character in your review like Suzy Menkes, or do you want to focus on reporting the collection as more of an omniscient narrator like Tim Blanks? How are you getting your reader into your review? Some strategies to consider are starting with a personal anecdote, submerging your reader in a detailed description of the scene, or grabbing your reader's attention with a catchy connection between the collection and popular culture. As demonstrated with the Menkes and Blanks examples, this is an area where your style as a writer can be established.

Your closing shouldn't be an afterthought. You want to leave the reader with something they'll remember, whether that's a final scene, a summarizing anecdote, or a question about where the designer is headed from here. Reading runway reports and seeing how your favourite fashion journalists handle them is a great way to understand the different ways to conclude.

Report or Review?

It might seem like semantics, but as with any art, there is a craft that comes with critique, and a critique is what is expected in a review. Depending on the experience and confidence of the writer as well as their knowledge of fashion as both an industry and a craft, a report might be more appropriate than a review.

As a writer, a report allows you to take it all in. With a review, there is an expectation of critique that requires more than "I like it" or "I don't like it." You'll be expected to support your assertions with evidence from the show just as you would with any persuasive piece of writing. You're essentially making an argument for your interpretation of the show, and that's why the report, rather than the review, is a good place to start for beginning fashion writers. It takes a great deal of knowledge and experience to back up a critique, though it holds far more weight for the outlet where it will appear and is far more valuable to the reader.

Today, live-streaming fashion shows and instant images on social media allow anyone with internet access to watch any of the shows at the Big Four (New York, Paris, London, Milan) fashion weeks (and others) from the comfort of their home no matter where in the world it is – Dubai, Shanghai, Berlin, or Austin. Fashion shows are more available and more accessible than ever, but it's how a fashion writer makes sense of a collection for others that really make the designer's story come to life.

As Diana Vreeland once said, "Fashion is part of the daily air and it changes all the time, with all the events. You can even see the approaching of a revolution in clothes. You can see and feel everything in clothes." By paying attention to not only what's on the runway but what's in the zeitgeist, a good runway report can communicate this for the reader.

Everything but Blank

Journalist Tim Blanks Talks About His Inspirations, Memorable Interviews, and How Fashion Is the Lifeblood of Humankind

At the time of this writing, seasoned journalist Tim Blanks is the editor-at-large for *Business of Fashion*. Blanks' past writing credits include some of the most influential titles in fashion, including *Vogue*, *GQ*, *Interview*, *Fantastic Man*, and *The Financial Times*. But truly it all began at *Fashion File*, a groundbreaking Canadian television show that took the audience behind the scenes of fashion and featured icons of the industry including Rei Kawakubo and Alexander McQueen.

As a fashion writer, Blanks is insightful, innovative, and always curious.

Who were the journalists and fashion writers when you were at the start of your career that you looked to? What was it about them that drew you to them? And did they have some of the same qualities in their work that you have developed over the years?

I give David Bowie credit for many things in my evolution, and so it was with the journalism that influenced me most, in particular the writers for English music mags and papers, people like Richard Williams, Ian MacDonald, Nick Kent, and Charles Shaar Murray. I osmosed everything they wrote about Bowie, and, by extension, everything else they covered, which is how I learned about bands like the Velvet Underground and the Stooges, and later, Roxy Music. I loved the passion, the humour, the obsessiveness, the partisanship of those writers, and the far-reaching connections they made to any – and everything.

The lens that you bring to your work is more layered than simply aesthetics – especially during this pandemic time. Of course, there is the artistry of design, but there are other factors (diversity, sustainability, representation, accessibility) that inform how you approach your work. Has that always been important to you? Was there space for that in fashion reporting prior to the past 5-ish years? How do you find it manifests in your writing?

Like I said, passion, obsession, and connectivity were things I took away from those writers I admired. If I didn't know a hell of a lot about fashion when I started writing about it, at least I knew it didn't exist in a vacuum. Ultimately, write about fashion and you're writing about the world. Just make sure you know about the world.

What would you say is the difference between reporting on fashion and reviewing it, especially when it comes to runway and collections? What is your perspective? What sets them apart from each other?

I've never felt I was a critic per se. Yes, I expressed my opinion, but I was more interested in conveying some sense of what it was like to be at a show, what it sounded like, moved like, smelt like. I guess that's reporting more than reviewing, but atmosphere was always so essential to what a designer was trying to communicate that it felt like the logical – and even sensitive – response to me [when it came to fashion shows].

What do you believe to be the role, and the responsibility, of fashion writing in terms of the industry and its ongoing "health"?

I don't colour fashion writing as the conscience of the industry, nothing as grandiose as that. It's an opportunity to celebrate artistry, ingenuity, and craftsmanship as well as the people who are responsible for them. It's also a chance to spotlight the facets of the industry that people are maybe not aware of. It does, after all, have an incredibly rich and largely unsung history, cast with wonderful characters and watershed moments that shaped culture. But it is also the second-biggest polluter, and it has only relatively recently begun to examine itself in the harsh light of human and environmental abuse. And there, as in any other art, writers, filmmakers, activists can call it to account.

You are an advocate for and champion of emerging designers in your writing. Why do you feel it's important for writers to cover the up-and-comers? How do you personally identify who is "worthy," and what is it about emerging designers that you find inspiring?

Without new talent, the industry has no future. I love finding new voices that speak to me. It's just like coming across a new actor who thrills me, or a fabulous writer I've not read before, or a musician I've not heard. I respond to vision, passion, originality, and maybe some kind of common ground or even a "I wish I could do that" yearning. I'm very partial to melancholy too, but that's something I personally enjoy in any artist's work. There's a lot of it in fashion, unsurprising in an industry at least partially based on the transience of beauty.

Is there a key element to fashion writing that would surprise people? Something unexpected but necessary to do the job well?

I think boundless curiosity is essential. And a sense of humour is critical. I can actually think of more elements that it would surprise you that you DON'T need than DO need.

What are the pieces that you have written that have stayed with you (in a positive way) throughout your career? Are there pieces that were a turning point for your voice? Maybe an emerging designer you championed or a show that you saw that blew your mind and changed how you saw fashion from there forward?

I have always had a rather cavalier approach to my fashion writing, possibly because I had to do so much of it in my years at style.com that it flowed through my fingers like water. So it's mostly people rather than pieces that stayed with me. Getting to write huge profiles of sphinxes like Helmut Lang, Linda Evangelista, Raf Simons, and Rei Kawakubo was obviously memorable. But I came to writing about fashion in a substantive way after a good 15 years of covering it on television so I think my voice was already pretty well-bedded in. And many of my most life-changing moments were during that 15 years, the Golden Age of fashion, and I rarely got to write about them. Actually, the turning points for my writer's voice were probably negative rather than positive, like when a bad review I wrote sparked a firestorm of controversy. I'm still banned from Celine.

Having worked in every medium, really (television, print, podcasts), what are the ways in which your coverage changes? Do you adjust what you're asking (if it's an interview) or how you provide commentary? Do you find that you need to curb your coverage, or places where you can be more prolific?

I could be completely trite and say I'm always me, whatever medium I'm working in. I'm curious about someone or something, and I explore that curiosity. Obviously, that requires research, and the research shapes my approach, but I don't let it bind me to preconceptions. I like talking to people, and I'm happy to follow the conversation where it leads. I've always been the bore at the dinner party who grills the guests. Perfect deflection, of course.

What have you found to be the most challenging part of your job? And how has that changed from when you first started to now?

Deadlines are an increasing challenge. I don't take on nearly as many assignments as I used to, but I seem to take longer delivering on them. It's especially tricky with the books I'm working on. To make matters worse, as I've got older, I've adopted a life's-too-short attitude. The world isn't going to end if my 2000 words on Matthew Williams isn't on someone's desk by EOD [end of day].

What motivates you as a writer/journalist?

Words. I love stringing them together to create different shapes. I had a really terrible drug experience a few years ago when I thought I was dying and it was literally chains of words I used to haul myself out of the darkness and back to the light of reason. That feeling of words saving me has stayed with me.

How did you get here? What captivates you about fashion? And are you where you thought you would be? Or envisioned yourself being? Are you ever still awestruck?

Fashion was a happy accident. I was looking for a full-time writing job, and *Toronto Life Fashion* happened to be the magazine that offered me one. So here I am 35 years later at *Business of Fashion*, after decades at *Fashion File* and style.com. My FAQ is probably "Don't you ever get bored watching shows?" Sure, after 8000 or so, there's been the odd moment, but there really is "always something else." I was back in Paris recently for the first time in two years, and there were at least three presentations that offered the most spectacular ripostes to the predations of the pandemic. You would not have seen them anywhere but in fashion because nowhere else would there be anyone using the artful alchemy of cloth and cut to express what we've been feeling for the past two years. And if that sounds like a tall order, it's precisely that which elevates fashion at its best to something that can border on the transcendent. I did say alchemy, didn't I? It's a kind of magic.

And finally, given what's happening in the fashion world right now, where will you be looking, and what will you be looking for as indicators of the future of fashion? How do you think it will impact covering fashion? Or will it?

Fashion is on its rims. The conglomerates are doing just fine for now, but an industry that is based on overproduction has an uncertain future if it is unable to make the changes that must happen now. I believe the commitment is there, but the challenges are so intertwined – less production means more unemployment, for instance – that I don't see a clear resolution for. Maybe a return to a world of dressmakers, tailors, and cobblers servicing their local communities, a celebration of human creativity, small scale, the way it used to be. Ultimately, fashion is in the blood of the species. It may shrink, but it will never die.

Notes

1. Mower, Sarah. "Saint Laurent Spring 2020 Ready-to-Wear Fashion Show." *Vogue*, 27 September 2019, www.vogue.com/fashion-shows/spring-2020-ready-to-wear/saint-laurent.
2. Elle UK. "All Aboard the Louis Vuiton Express with Marc Jacobs." *Elle UK*, 7 March 2012, www.elle.com/uk/fashion/news/a7597/all-aboard-the-louis-vuitton-express-with-marc-jacobs/.
3. Mower, Sarah. "Mary Kantrantzou." *Vogue*, 16 February 2019, www.vogue.com/fashion-shows/fall-2019-ready-to-wear/mary-katrantzou
4. Blanks, Tim. "At Tom Ford, Echoes of Collections Past." *The Business of Fashion*, 6 September 2018, www.businessoffashion.com/articles/fashion-show-review/at-tom-ford-echoes-of-collections-past.
5. Menkes, Suzy. "#SuzyNYFW: Tom Ford – Seducing Clients As Much As The Camera." *British Vogue*, 7 September 2018, www.vogue.co.uk/article/suzynyfw-tom-ford-seducing-clients-as-much-as-the-camera.

Annotated Bibliography

Agins, Teri. *The End of Fashion: How Marketing Changed the Clothing Business Forever.* Harper Collins, 2001.
  Wall Street Journal reporter Teri Agins here explores the impact of mass marketing on the fashion industry. This book explores mass marketing's effects through many aspects of the fashion industry, including manufacturing, retailing, financing, and image making.

Browne, Alix. *Runway: The Spectacle of Fashion.* Rizzoli Publications, 2016.
  This book focuses on the runway show as a form of entertainment and creativity as important as the fashion itself, and on fashion designers for whom spectacle plays an important role. Including never-before-published photos, this text showcases the most notable high-fashion runway shows of the past two decades.

Geczy, Adam, and Vicki Karaminas. *Fashion Installation: Body, Space, and Performance.* Bloomsbury Visual Arts, 2019.
  A critical exploration of the changing means of fashion exhibition. This book aims to contextualize the fashion installation, focusing on innovative fashion exhibitions and their designers historically today.

Luvaas, Brent. *Street Style: An Ethnography of Fashion Blogging.* Bloomsbury Publishing, 2016.
  Street Style documents the rise and influence of amateur, American street style photography and fashion blogging on the global fashion industry. Street style photography is here explored as a powerful form of amateur ethnography.

Voss, Kimberly Wilmot. *Newspaper Fashion Editors in the 1950s and 60s: Women Writers of the Runway.* Palgrave Macmillan, 2021.
  Kimberly Wilmot Voss analyzes the social, economic, and political dimensions of fashion, addressing fashion show reporting, journalism ethics, and the contents of newspaper fashion sections following World War II. This book positions soft news and fashion journalism as valuable and important.

Werle, Simone. *Style Diaries: World Fashion from Berlin to Tokyo.* Prestel, 2010.
  This book showcases the personal style and viewpoints of more than 40 fashion bloggers, offering access and insight into influential fashion forces. Insightful, accessible, and fully illustrated.

Williams, K., et al., editors. *Fashion, Design and Events* (1st ed.). Routledge, 2013.
  An edited volume that explores Western fashion and design events from a social perspective in order to analyze and critique issues of gender, identity, commodification, and authenticity. This book brings needed context to an under researched topic.

Wolbers, Marian Frances. *Uncovering Fashion: Fashion Communications Across the Media.* Fairchild Books, 2009.
  This book focuses on key areas of the fashion industry in order to reveal its underlying network of communications. Using a systematic approach, this text explores the wide range of media and processes that make up the field of fashion communication.

5 Don't Get Left Behind
Trend Reports and Service Pieces

While the runway shows embody the glamour of the fashion world in the public eye, it is the trends that are the everyday workhorses. The average individual interested in fashion is generally concerned with *how* they might recreate some of the magic exhibited on the runway in their own daily lives. This is where trends come in. Trends are the takeaway message of the season, and they fuel fashionistas and fashion retailers alike.

This chapter covers the trend report and its fraternal twin, the service piece. The trend report is a mainstay of fashion writing. It's where you, as a fashion journalist, get to translate the key concepts seen on the runway while helping the average person get dressed.

A trend report advises readers on the key trends for the upcoming season. The trend report can be a great indicator of how much attention the writer is paying because trends don't just come from designers and the annual cycle of fashion shows; they come from contemporary culture, the street, and other elements of the zeitgeist. For example, popular culture frequently sparks trends, like the corset whether it's courtesy of '90s Madonna or the Mr. Pearl corset worn by Kim Kardashian to the 2019 Met Gala.

The Corset

The corset is an item that exemplifies the way a historical garment can be transformed repeatedly by popular culture into a trend. While the term "corset" can be found back to the 14th century, the corset "as we've become familiar with" became popular in the 16th century. As aesthetics and trends changed, the corset moved in and out of fashion. By the end of World War II, corsets were no longer standard elements of a women's wardrobe.

Corsets regained popularity briefly in the '50s with the "Merry Widow," which nipped in the waist and separated the breasts. From then on, the corset became predominantly an item of fetish wear. It is this history that helped fuel the controversy caused by the corset designed by Jean Paul

DOI: 10.4324/9781003047629-8

> Gaultier worn by Madonna on her *Blond Ambition* tour in 1990. Fast-forward 30 years, and the corset sees a revival through the television series *Bridgerton*. A deeper consideration of the corset can be found in Valerie Steele's book *The Corset: A Cultural History*.

Trends aren't necessarily something handed down from on high (i.e. designers); they're the result of a conversation that's happening at the moment all around. The zeitgeist, "spirit of the times," has been mentioned in both the Introduction as well as Chapter 1, and trends are an embodiment of that. Have you ever pulled an item from the back of your closet and immediately been transported to when and where you wore it? Were you able to recall everything that was going on in your life and the world at large when you put it on? Trends are a way of communicating the collective unconsciousness of an era.

The service piece takes the trend report and makes it instructional. It shows you how to make the most of a trend by providing tips on how to incorporate it into your existing wardrobe. It frequently shows you how to wear it; for example, whenever scarves or shawls reappear in fashion, there is an opportunity to demonstrate ways to style them that make them fresh or current.

Trend Spotting

Since every season has multiple trends, and these are not disseminated through a centralized system, how do you figure out what they will be?

Take a look around you. What is in the air? How is the collective consciousness, or zeitgeist, manifesting around you? During the pandemic, it became de rigueur to wear masks that were then interpreted by the fashion industry. We also witnessed the resurgence of loungewear, which, too, has made it out of the comfort of our homes and onto the street. There are a number of places where trends incubate. Be alert to possibilities.

As we've mentioned already, a prime location for trends is the runway. The reporting from the annual showing of collections used to be the main way people found out what the trends were for the upcoming season. In those days, shows were attended mostly by journalists and buyers for shops. The journalists took note of key pieces or looks and distilled them down into trends for the general population. If possible, they paid attention to what the buyers were responding to as well as an indication of what was going to be hitting the shelves soon. Even in this rarefied environment, there was a conversation happening. This conversation is now even bigger.

It is not just the big houses whose runways warrant attention; it is also the smaller shows put on by independent designers, who may be housed together under a combined umbrella, as well as the graduate shows mounted by fashion school programmes. Central Saint Martins has a fashion programme that has been long celebrated for the designers whose talent it has fostered including Alexander

McQueen, Stella McCartney, and Hussein Chalayan. The MA (Master's degree) fashion show is part of London Fashion Week and can be an excellent source of upcoming trends. There are fashion design programmes all over the world; Central Saint Martins is just one of many schools in London. Other notable schools include the Fashion Institute of Technology (FIT) in New York City; the Royal Academy of Fine Arts in Antwerp, Belgium; the Bunka Fashion College in Tokyo, Japan; and the Ecole de la Chambre Syndicale de la Couture Parisienne in Paris. But established schools are not the only fertile ground for discovering trends. Do a little research, and see if any of your local universities or colleges have fashion programmes. You may be surprised by the innovation on display.

Press days are another way to view a collection. Runway shows are expensive to put on, and not every label can afford them or wants to take that route, so press days are scheduled for buyers and fashion journalists during fashion week. These are more intimate affairs that are primarily focused on the garments. They more closely resemble the original fashion shows of the early 1900s.

Popular culture is a site for exploration when looking for trends. We've already touched on the corset, but popular culture goes beyond music or television. Mass media – communication that reaches and potentially influences a large group of people – includes not only television and music but also film, print and online media (newspapers, magazines, online publications), and radio. Make sure to include the reading of newspapers and magazines as well as paying attention to the news in general part of your routine; it will help you make connections that signal an upcoming trend.

Social media, in recent years, has been a very prolific arena for the birth of trends. The rise of the influencer has transformed what had previously been a simple sharing of selfies into a dissemination of trends and ideas. Most influencers do not actually define trends; they're more likely to be showcasing them on behalf of a label or a store. Nonetheless, they will frequently be in the now before the trend hits the magazine stands, so finding a few influencers to follow will help you in your search.

Social media is also great for seeing what people are wearing on the street. It used to be that trends trickled down from the runway to the street, but now smart fashion journalists pay heed to what is being worn outside the tent as well as what's being shown inside. Designers themselves have looked to street style for inspiration for their collections. This is another example of the back-and-forth conversation happening in the moment.

As with social media influencers, celebrities are frequently ahead of the game when it comes to trends. Pay attention to what is seen on the red carpet during award season. Notice if multiple celebrities are suddenly spotted wearing a certain shoe, a style of denim, or carrying a new bag. Just because a celebrity wears something doesn't necessarily mean it's a trend, but it can be a good indicator of them.

One more area of popular culture that may inspire trends are museum shows. In Chapter 1, we discussed museum shows as being a way to understand fashion history and its context. They are also a good place to get some clues as to what trends might be making their debut in the coming season. Museums around the world have been mounting exhibitions featuring either the work of a single designer, such as the Alexander McQueen show *Savage Beauty*, or the work of multiple designers combined under the umbrella of a common aesthetic or style, such as *Kimono: From Kyoto to Catwalk*, which provided both a historical background for the kimono and contemporary designers' interpretation of it. Frequently, these shows travel to different institutions around the globe. *David Bowie Is* was one such exhibition, and it's an interesting example as it is not centered around designers but around a musical icon. It's a meeting of popular culture with fashion. This show included photographs and ephemera from his life and career but was particularly popular because it showcased many of his iconic fashions. The show opened at the Victoria and Albert Museum in London in March 2013 and visited ten other museums before closing at the Brooklyn Museum in New York City in April 2018, five years later. Some of the trends during the run of this exhibitions held commonalities with Bowie's fashion sense such as the jumpsuit/all-in-one (a trend in 2014) and the suit (2017).

A final source for information on upcoming trends is forecasting agencies. These are professionals whose job is to predict upcoming trends. Generally used by designers and marketing professionals, trend forecasting agencies cull the vast amount of information at hand, through research and algorithms, to pinpoint key trends – both short-term and long-term. Not only analysing hard data, such as spending habits and economic indicators, but also looking at influencers, street style icons, and blogs, trend forecasting agencies work to predict predilections in colour, fabrics, and style, which they make available to clients for a fee.

The Object of Desire

So, let's say you've been paying attention, have caught a number of runway shows, and are seeing some items or aesthetic ideas repeated. These could be your trends, but how do you define them for your readers? The following steps should help take your trend report from forgettably generic to memorably specific.

The first thing you need to do is to define the trend. A trend doesn't have to be a brand-new style; they're often reworkings of older looks, so be on the lookout for fashions that have come around again. A trend can be a subtle shift in cut or colour. It can also be a re-envisioning of the proper occasion or environment for an item. Witness the trend frenzy caused by Sharon Stone when she wore a Gap turtleneck to the Oscars in 1996. It wasn't the cut or colour of the turtleneck that ignited interest; it was the idea of wearing a mass-market item typically designated as casual wear to one of the most watched red carpets. Fast-forward to the 2021 Oscars when director Chloé Zhao's white sneakers sparked another trend that shifted the focus from object to occasion.

There are numerous ways to define a trend. A trend can be based on a type of fabric like velvet or corduroy. It can be focused on a colour, or it can be centred around a cut, such as wide-legged trousers, which have been in and out of fashion since the '20s.

> ### Fashion Colour Trend Report From Pantone
>
> Since 2016, Pantone has been publishing the Fashion Colour Trend Report. In 2017, they began to put together separate colour stories for the New York and London Fashion Weeks (both fall/winter and spring/summer). These reports feature "a colour overview highlighting the top colours fashion designers . . . will be featuring in their collections for the upcoming season." The reports start with a brief narrative of the mood and feeling of the upcoming season and then connect the featured colours with the Pantone equivalents. These trend reports frequently but not always feature Pantone's Color of the Year, which itself is the result of *"Pantone's color experts at the Pantone Color Institute™ comb(ing) the world looking for new color influences. These can include the entertainment industry and films in production, traveling art collections and new artists, fashion, all areas of design, popular travel destinations, as well as new lifestyles, playstyles, and socio-economic conditions. Influences may also stem from new technologies, materials, textures, and effects that impact color, relevant social media platforms and even upcoming sporting events that capture worldwide attention."*

It can also highlight a specific part of the body. Off-the-shoulder looks have been on trend on and off for years. The most contemporary iteration may take its inspiration from Donna Karan's 1992 cut-out shoulder dress, which was nicknamed "The Cold Shoulder Dress." As Donna Karan herself told the *New York Times*, one of the appeals of this style is that most everyone can wear it: "It's the one place that looks perfect on every woman's body. No one ever says, 'I have fat shoulders.'"[1] The cold-shoulder look made a recent public appearance when the singer Dolly Parton wore one to get her COVID-19 vaccine.

Frequently, there is an "it" item for the season. These "trophy items," as they're also known, are often accessories, which by being designated a trend become very difficult to find. Be on the lookout for items such as shoes styles that are repeated, jewellery that appears prominent, or very specific styles of hats or handbags. As with many designer goods, the price tags of these items will generally be high, but they often have attainable counterparts in mainstream shops and the high street.

Not Just a Physical Thing

Another way you can define a trend is through a more thematic lens. You may find that a certain period of history is making a comeback whether it's through an interpretation of Regency-era fashion or a new version of the '20s flapper. This often coincides with the release of a major film production or a highly touted television series, as we've already demonstrated with our sidebar on the corset.

A particular aesthetic or style may be the trend. It needn't always be about the physical garments. It could be a return to minimalism or a desire to return to times that seemed freer or more relaxed as embodied through a bohemian look. The zeitgeist can definitely push a particular aesthetic to the forefront. If people are feeling that the world is not a safe place or there are armed conflicts making the news, military chic may be on trend because the clothing can suggest a certain rugged utility that is desired. Again, having a larger understanding of the world at large when trend spotting is invaluable.

One more area where a trend may be born is in the way an item is worn. Whether it's sporting the price tag, wearing something backwards or over something unexpected, or simply tying a cardigan differently, a trend can be how something familiar has been reinvigorated through a novel way of wearing it.

Say My Name

Once you've defined a trend, try to think of a catchy name for it. Remember, a trend is something that's new and exciting, so calling it "the long dress" trend may not inspire interest or curiosity. It also lacks descriptive panache. However, calling it "the prairie dress" trend, for instance, immediately separates it from other maxi dresses and conjures up a specific aesthetic. If a name sticks in a reader's mind, it's likely to get traction.

Watch for microtrends as well. As demonstrated through the trend pyramid, there are multiple layers to trends, which are generally defined by their staying power. Often one will have lost sight of the megatrend, which, by a certain point, becomes a dominant aspect (as defined by cultural theorist Raymond Williams and touched upon in Chapter 1) of society. For example, responding to climate change doesn't necessarily feel like a trend, but it's a megatrend, which has become a fact of life for many.

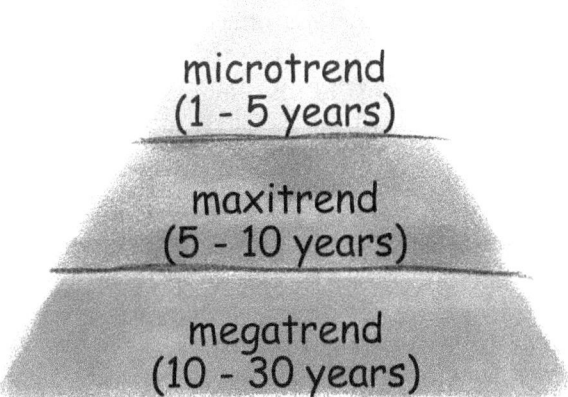

Figure 5.1 Trend Pyramid
Source: Courtesy of Ian A. Manley

For example, let's say you've noticed a growing use of leather alternatives, and in one season, you find multiple examples of faux leather made from mushrooms. It isn't necessarily everywhere, but it's prevalent enough to warrant attention. This could be considered a microtrend. Its life span may be only a season, or it can resonate for years. The maxitrend this is an outgrowth of is the ongoing conversation about sustainability in fashion, which itself is linked to the megatrend of environmental awareness.

Putting Pen to Paper

You've already started the work of writing a trend report by defining and naming it. As with every piece of writing, make sure the trend report you're working on will be of interest to your readers. Crop tops may not be of interest to readers of a magazine dedicated to women over 50 or women in conservative countries.

After you've defined the trend for your readers, you need to explicate why it's big this season. This may be where you add a bit of historical background to give it a larger context. In general, you will not spend a lot of time on this as the real reason for a trend report is to encourage your readers to take it up themselves.

Explain why readers should want to try the trend. It may be that an item is universally flattering or doesn't require a certain kind of body to wear (see our discussion of the "cold-shoulder" look earlier in this chapter). You may be able to create enthusiasm by suggesting readers already own items that could recreate these looks.

To create interest, tell them where it's been spotted. Most people do not want to buy into a trend until they know it's been vetted by either the fashion community at large or celebrities. Being able to provide images of famous people sporting the trend adds credibility to your piece. Depending on your demographic, you may also want to include images of the trend on the street. Influencers and street style favourites can do a lot to help launch a trend.

It helps to detail how a trend has made the transition from the runway to the local boutique. Provide readers with not only the original items that spawned the trend but also the items they may be more readily able to access or afford.

A trend report doesn't have to always flow in the aforementioned manner. Think about what your audience will respond to. While this may not be an option for you as a fashion writer, having two people try out the trend in real life, preferable one who loves the trend and another who disdains it, can be an engaging way to cover it. Depending upon the publication, this may very well fit with their demographic. "Worn in real life" pieces can make for a compelling copy. They build upon the idea that fashion is for everyone because everyone needs to get dressed. While this may feel like it veers into service piece territory, it is more of a practical test drive performed by individuals the readers would respond to. Understanding, for example, the pros and cons of a chunky-heeled boot in daily life may sway a reader better than images of celebrities in them.

Both the trend report and the service piece have a degree of prediction that is expected by editors. You should point to what's coming next, not simply dwell on the trends with which the readers are already familiar. You'll need to do some research as well as talk with fashion industry experts. Try to anticipate what the readers want (i.e. to be both on and ahead of the trends) and understand why.

A good service piece has a clear call to action. What do your readers need to know in order to act on your suggestions? You'll need to demonstrate solid reporting skills here. This is not an opinion piece, but an article with a theory (i.e. here's a trend you should try) backed by evidence (i.e. because it's flattering/age-appropriate/unexpected/etc.), which can be provided through your references to its provenance and where it's been seen (i.e. on the runway or celebrity).

The trend report can act as the framework for the service piece. You've established the presence of this trend and now can add details on how to wear or utilize it. Oftentimes, this will require a reproportioning of specific elements such as cutting back the historical background to make room for the service portion. Define the trend and give reasons why readers should try it, and then follow up by providing examples of how to wear or style it.

The trend report and service piece both should demonstrate strong writing skills that speak to a specific audience. You may begin with your instincts, sharply honed by practice, but then you'll need to move towards an idea that is supported by the evidence, which is all around you.

Moda With Mower

British Fashion Critic Sarah Mower Explains Her Journalist Journey and Why Emerging Designers Are Always the Future

Sarah Mower is direct, decisive, and determined to call it like she sees it in an industry often filled with effusive interviews and sugar-coated reviews. As an advocate for emerging British fashion talent, she has covered some of today's greats while in their infancy including Erdem, JW Anderson, and Simone Rocha.

Mower's career began in the early '80s at *Ms London* magazine, followed by a fashion editor position at *The Guardian*. Her career credits to date include *Harper's Bazaar US*, *Vogue*, and *The Times*. Today she is chief critic at vogue.com. And for her contributions to fashion journalism, Mower was awarded the Member of the British Empire in 2011.

When do you think an interest in fashion begins?
What I've observed is that most people in fashion, whether designers, stylists, or journalists, usually started studying without knowing it from the age of 9 or 10. Playing with dolls, teddies, Barbies, dressing up, watching mothers,

sisters, brothers, grandmothers – all this goes to form people's fashion consciousness.

Martin Margiela played with Barbies and customized them. Alber Elbaz dressed his parents' chess pieces. Jean Paul Gaultier made a corset for his teddy. Erdem made dresses for his twins' Skipper doll – everyone has their own story.

When did it start for you?

For me, it was watching my granny who loved making clothes, being given history books, and taken to museums, galleries, and castles in England and Wales. I was brought up in Bath, which is a Roman city with hot baths, rebuilt as a spa town in Georgian times, so we were surrounded by layers and layers of history. My first ambition was to be an archaeologist. To some extent, I think I am an archaeologist of fashion too, because knowing your history – or rather, how to unpick and question history – is the other prerequisite for being able to write about fashion. You have to start off being able to make comparisons, or to be alert to the fact that you should look for them.

Where did you discover your interest in fashion and criticism?

Growing up, I was incredibly lucky that there is a brilliant Museum of Fashion in Bath. I spent hours on end there, absorbing the differences between pannier dresses, the empire line, bustles, crinolines, and bias-cut gowns – I suppose that gave me the idea that clothes are part of social history and to ask why they looked like that. It resulted in my always picturing exactly what people must have been wearing during the times I was learning about in school history lessons, so every project on Elizabeth 1, the Vikings, or Celtic civilization was returned fully illustrated.

I did look at my parents' newspaper, *The Daily Telegraph*. I think it must have been Ernestine Carter, but I didn't read her pieces – I looked at the drawings, illustrating her reports from the couture shows in the '60s. And then I started making fashion drawings, with swatches and collaged fabric ladies. My mother was an art teacher, so I was incredibly lucky. I still have them. "By Sarah Mower aged 9 ½."

Another stroke of luck was that we had a wealthy aunt who swooped down one day when I was drawing in a corner and decided to give me a year's subscription to *Vogue* for my 12th birthday, which was a massive thing for me – again, I can only remember the pictures.

Now, from interviewing so many designers, I know it's normal to begin that way – it's like being obsessed with a sport or music or anything else that forms you for life. This is why I have always understood that it doesn't matter where you come from – it's what you take in from who's around you, the culture you absorb, and that pays you back for ever. It's not about having money or a privileged background. In the UK it's really noticeable that all but one or two designers went to state school. The components of talent in fashion are many and various, and they can't be bought. It is about who you are as an individual.

Anything that teaches you to observe in detail is good, and so is being a bit of an outsider. It gives you distance. I was fat and laughed at for my illustrated essays at school. That's not an unusual experience – it might actually be a qualification – because fashion is made up of people who were misunderstood weirdos as kids.

I never thought for one second that there was a career ahead for me in fashion or any branch of it. It really didn't occur to me or my parents or teachers, and I do think that had I suggested it, my parents would have been horrified. Needlework at the convent school I went to was reserved for girls who were regarded as slower (and I hated it). I was good at English, history, and art, so that's the way I went – to Leeds University to study English and the history of art. This was the time of punk and New Wave when fashion was out of fashion. I was taught by the feminist art historian Griselda Pollock, which was a big thing. Learning to see and to be able to dissect imagery as political constructs, and to question how narratives are written, is a fundamental grounding. As soon as it was obvious that women artists had been and continued to be ignored by history and the entire art system – well, that was fuel to the fire of criticism.

Have you found there's a commonality amongst designers when it comes to inspiration?

Designers these days name-drop like crazy while discussing their references and pointing at boards: the names of artists (the more obscure the better), arcane films, music. That's easy to research instantly now – but again, fashion isn't just a jigsaw puzzle of claimed references. Slavishly reporting the designer's inspirations can be a trap, or a distraction from the fact that it's just a mediocre piece of work.

How did your work in fashion journalism begin?

My actual 'break' into fashion journalism was sheer accident. While I was doing my finals, I bought the only copy of *Vogue* which was on the student union newsstand and went in for "The Vogue Talent Contest" – just to distract myself from the fear of exams. I remember writing a review of a Helmut Newton book and a German Neue Sachlichkeit exhibition.

Next thing I was a finalist at a *Vogue* lunch, which was truly terrifying. I was runner-up. The girl who won was, strangely enough, the niece of a Thatcher cabinet minister, so I didn't get the internship. Instead, I got a job at a free magazine for young women called *Ms London* – an amazing way to start because it was produced in one room in Fleet Street, so I learned about all the processes of commissioning, subbing, photoshoots, and layouts as well as being thrown in the deep end to put together my own weekly page. It wasn't all fashion, but suddenly, I was a journalist, covering London shopping ideas, exhibitions, book reviews, club-style reports, and interviews with new designers.

This is another thing I always pass on to students. If I'd been taken into *Vogue*, I would probably have spent those two years in a cupboard in the fashion department or running errands for the features editors, and I suspect I'd never have survived that. For your first steps, try to work for a small to medium-size company where you can learn how things are done and are likely to be thrown work when it's a question of everyone pitching in to meet a deadline.

When I look at the work I was doing then, it was always about emerging designers, only I was the same age as them. I think it's good to remember who you were at 23 – I felt grown up and full of ideas, mostly anti-establishment ones. Today, older people continually underestimate the intelligence and capabilities of young people and often actively put them down. I've always thought that's incredibly stupid. I've never forgotten all the women who gave me a chance in my career; they, with all their different character traits, are my role models. Not that I ever thought in terms of "role model."

I'm really only interested in how fashion represents society and how designers reflect it – whether that's deliberately or unconsciously because there is no way of escaping being in our time.

What do you believe to be the role, and the responsibility, of fashion writing?

As far as criticism is concerned, I've always wanted my writing to be understandable by people who aren't specialists and insiders. As in any kind of reporting or criticism, be it film, theatre, art, there is nothing worse than obfuscating name-dropping. I don't always come up to my own mark, but I think the goal is to describe and explain what you are seeing in the neatest number of words. Clichés and fashion-isms are terrible, too – I have a banned list. The exciting and difficult part is trying not to fall back on your own formulae. I am constantly trying to check myself.

The hardest part is to write the first sentence because if you don't get that right, no one's going to read further.

Not only does your work have a clear POV, but the lens is far more layered than simply aesthetics. Of course, there is the artistry of design, but there are other factors (diversity, sustainability, representation, accessibility) that inform how you approach your work. Has that always been important to you, and how do you find it manifests in your writing?

In the past decade, it's become increasingly obvious that all the windows we've been looking through in fashion have been facing in one direction – at a landscape conditioned by white western male narratives. My own education was faulty, almost completely lacking in anything to do with colonial history. Even when discussing Victorian history and the Industrial Revolution, we learned and were shocked and outraged by the conditions in cotton mills in the North of England – but never asked to know any of the reality of where cotton came from, and why.

The decolonization of fashion, fashion history, and writing is only just beginning. It's becoming obvious that the whole architecture of it must be rebuilt and that the colonial routes of oppression and exploitation are still very much in operation in the supply chains of clothing manufacturing, and of course, destruction of the environment.

So, "diversity" in the design and representation of fashion is the most important and revolutionary development there is in this century. I am learning from so many young designers and journalists and realizing that studying the background of what they talk about is crucial to trying to have an understanding. Grace Wales Bonner, Kerby Jean-Raymond, Nicholas Daley, Priya Ahluwalia, Bianca Saunders are outstanding in this new generation. The most important thing now is that communicators come up alongside them to amplify and explain what they do and are saying. Critics and writers are always involved in art, cultural, and political movements; they also make the debate grow within communities, emboldening and encouraging more voices to speak – as well as waking up the mainstream.

This goes for people from every community I can think of.

"Sustainability" – there's a contentious word. Today, there is a journalistic responsibility to ask, and a responsibility from manufacturers and brands to say how they made their clothes. In the format of reviews, in the time that we've historically had to write (within 3 hours of the show, in the old frantic schedule), it's hard to probe. But I will say that far more questions are being asked of designers about fabric content and the carbon footprint involved with shows and shipping. Companies know that they can be taken down for environmental misdeeds – hence the rise of greenwashing. Again, having your antennae alert to this is the key and self-education. Then it all comes down to speaking in clear language about it.

The whole area is hedged around by acronyms and untangling them is a tricky task. The best way, I find, is to give designers who are practising well as much airtime as you can – they make it intelligible. I get the best out of breaking down the issues by interviewing Stella McCartney, Gabriella Hearst, Maggie Marilyn, and Greg Lauren. I also constantly learn from Fashion Revolution and from Celine Semaan of Slow Factory, whose global connectedness is phenomenal.

You have been a vocal and active supporter of emerging designers and young voices in fashion. What unique perspectives do they bring that more established designers may not?

Why am I interested in what young people think? It's curiosity, to start with. I can't stand not to know what the next movement is going to be. Students, graduates, emerging designers are always the shapers of the future. It is much, much more interesting to me to be able to spend time talking with students than interviewing established designers who inevitably have the same things to say.

A different role grew out of that. Having observed all the problems that new designers have, I decided that I should help them, representing their problems to the British Fashion Council (BFC) and lobbying for funds and mentoring. There comes a point in your career where you know so many people, and about so many pitfalls, that you should use that knowledge to make things better. When the financial crash came in 2008/9, I was afraid a generation would be wiped out. The BFC gave me the title of Ambassador for Emerging Talent, and together we built a ladder of support in London. It includes a scholarship fund – the first recipient was Erdem.

Given what has happened over the past several years in fashion, where will you be looking to get a picture of the future of fashion?

We're all facing an even more monstrous problem than the crash. It would be foolish to predict how the pandemic will change fashion, but it can't carry on with the volume of shows and the overproduction it was perpetrating "before." In my career, I've witnessed over decades how fashion is shaped by the movements of economies, foreign exchange rates, booms, busts, politics, and protest movements. What I know is that people, especially creative people, always adapt. For me, despite the fear, the job of an observer is just the same: to search out and highlight the people who are coming up with forms of clothing that have purpose and function and are imbued with social, intellectual, and emotional meaning. In a different world order, all I will say is that it's more likely that coalitions of smaller people will be able to do that than giant conglomerates. That's the hope that keeps me going.

Note

1 Rubenstein, Hal. *Thing: Cold Shoulder*. New York Times, 7 February 1993.

Work Cited

Rubenstein, Hal. Thing: Cold Shoulder. *New York Times*, 7 February 1993.

Annotated Bibliography

Bradford, Julie. *Fashion Journalism*. Routledge, 2014.
   A guide to effective and responsible fashion journalism, this book includes theory, research, and interviews with journalists, editors, bloggers, and others. This revised second edition explores the changes within the fashion industry and their meanings for fashion journalism.

Cope, Jon, and Dennis Maloney. *Fashion Promotion in Practice*. Bloomsbury Publishing, 2016.
   A guide to fashion promotion that includes exercises, case studies, and interviews with fashion industry professionals, exploring issues such as catwalk democratization, brand collaborations, public relations, and campaign planning. This illustrated, accessible text explores contemporary promotional practice in a way applicable to utilization in prospective campaigns.

Divita, Lorynn. *Fashion Forecasting*. Fairchild Books, 2019.
   A guide to anticipating emerging fashion trends, preparing and presenting fashion forecasts. Complete with a new appendix, new influencer profiles, and three new chapters.

Miller, Sanda, and Peter McNeil. *Fashion Journalism: History, Theory, and Practice*. Bloomsbury Publishing, 2018.

A comprehensive how-to guide to fashion journalism that includes global case studies and exercises designed to develop critical and analytical writing skills. This accessible book is designed to improve writing in many styles, including blogging, art reviews, interviews, and more.

Swanson, Kristen K., and Judith C. Everett. *Writing for the Fashion Business*. Fairchild, 2008. Designed to help students practise writing and critical thinking, this textbook includes real-world examples and case studies and discusses form and content issues in relation to fashion writing. This book is designed to bridge the gap between general writing instruction and upper-level fashion writing courses.

6 Do You See What I See?
Fashion Beyond Fashion

Sometimes you want to get further into an idea, or perhaps a current trend reminds you of something you've read or seen, and you're inspired to dig deeper. You may recall that earlier in *Fashion Writing: A Primer* we advised you to pay attention to contemporary culture and news beyond fashion in order to be able to write about fashion in a larger context. Unlike the runway report or the service piece, the feature provides more room (aka word count) available for you to explore.

A runway report, trend report, or service piece each has as its primary function to give the reader an opportunity to visualize the clothes as well as develop an understanding of how to wear them. The feature is a longer piece whose function can change depending upon what you wish to communicate.

Most of the writing we've done so far has had a limited word count. Trend reports are more often than not in the 500- to 1000-word count range. A runway review frequently tops out somewhere around 1000 words, depending on the media outlet. A feature is distinguished not only by its length, however, but also by its focus.

While not necessarily reliant on the daily news cycle, the feature still needs to be recognizable as newsworthy. The feature goes beyond reportage. It allows you to flex your creative muscle. Feature writing responds to the human interest story behind fashion. It often includes personal reflections on current events or interviews with people of interest. Feature writing exists in a dynamic relationship with the zeitgeist.

> ### The Fashion and Race Database
>
> Begun in 2016, the goal of the Fashion and Race Database is "to center and amplify the voices of those who have been racialized (and thus marginalized) in fashion, illuminate under-examined histories and address racism throughout the fashion system." The database is organized into six distinct sections: The Library, the most widely used section, features scholarly essays, reading lists, documentaries, and more; Objects That Matter focuses on fashion objects, images, and collections that have been excluded

DOI: 10.4324/9781003047629-9

> from fashion history and museums and examines their implications and impact; Profiles highlights racialized people who have impacted the fashion world; Essays & News features original content that focuses on the voices of racialized scholars, students, and others; The Directory provides resources to connect with others working in this area; and The Calendar highlights global events and conversations centring on race and fashion.

A feature could be something as clear as a profile of a fashion figure: "Meet Aditi Mayer, the sustainability activist decolonising fashion, one Instagram post at a time,"[1] or it can be something as esoteric as "On the Uses and Abuses of Benjamin for Thinking About Fashion,"[2] which references the philosopher and writer Walter Benjamin. It can be a deeper dive into the inspiration behind one of the season's hot trends. You might look at how fashion affects a specific group of people or perhaps the impact of fashion beyond the body.

In this chapter, we'll discuss the basics of feature writing as well as show you some other places (genres) where fashion writing can come into play such as creative nonfiction, fiction, and scriptwriting.

Where You Lead

Features, whether about fashion or another subject, all follow a similar structure. There will be an opening (also known as a lede) that is designed to grab the reader's attention and interest. This is where knowing your audience (Chapter 3) comes in. What will they respond to? Why are they reading *this* publication, and what do they expect? The answer to these and other questions will help you decide how to start your piece.

> *It is not surprising that a handbag should figure so prominently in the film chronicling Margaret Thatcher's legacy – a sprawling tale brought to the big screen by Meryl Streep in The Iron Lady. This personal carry-all has long been both functional and symbolic. Depending on its style and brand, it can be a statement of status or a pronouncement of folksiness. Hand it off to a hen-pecked husband or a put-upon assistant and it can demean or belittle. A purse can impress and intimidate, bewilder, berate, or amuse.*[3]

Follow your opener with a paragraph that explains what the piece is all about. Sometimes, as demonstrated by the previous examples, a piece starts with a story or a quick scene, which builds interest but doesn't necessarily tell you what the piece is about. For example, you might open your feature on the role of footwear in the modern fashionista's life with a personal anecdote about ruining your new shoes in an unexpected downpour. In the next paragraph, you'd connect this to what essentially is the thesis (main idea) of your feature. In our example, let's say it's "Contemporary shoe designers have finally come on board with beautiful shoes that are still functional."

This paragraph also serves as what is called the nut (US English) or the nub (UK English) paragraph. You're going to explain to the readers why this is newsworthy now. Newsworthiness can be based on what's making news, what television show/movie/song is currently popular, or an exciting collaboration. The important thing here is for the reader to recognize its newsworthiness. Why should the reader care, and why do they care now?

> **Protest Movements**
>
> From the Arab Spring (2010–2012[4]), to Idle No More[5] (2012–present), to Black Lives Matter (2013–present), the past decade has seen protest movements gain strength across the globe. Millions of people have taken to the streets to make their voices heard and their governments more responsive. In 2019 alone, there were major protests in Hong Kong, Algeria, The Sudan, Chile, and many other countries. The focus on the protests ranges from policing issues, systemic racism, and lack of basic human rights to tax hikes, corrupt leadership, and authoritarian regimes. The prevalence of social media has been a factor in many of these movements gaining both momentum and recognition in the media.

The bulk of your feature will be a further exploration of your subject. If we are using shoes as our subject, you might be discussing collaborations between designers and athletic companies or the return of the Birkenstock to the runway. As long as you can make it interesting and relevant to your reader (again, know your audience), you can write about it.

Many features require research – both primary and secondary. Primary research sources are first-hand accounts; for example, you might interview a shoe designer or the head of research and development (R&D) at an athletic company. You could visit a factory or an atelier and see for yourself the process from start to finish. Secondary research sources are pretty much anything that has been filtered or reported by someone else initially. They are a step removed from primary sources and are generally written by someone who didn't experience the subject first-hand. They frequently analyse or interpret primary sources.

Finally, as with any other piece of writing, you want a solid conclusion that helps to tie things together and leave the reader satisfied or curious enough to continue exploring the subject further. Don't undermine all the work that went into your feature with a flat ending.

Come Together

A feature is not an academic essay, but it does have a beginning, a middle, and an end. Unlike a news story, which follows an inverted pyramid structure that starts with the who, what, where, and when of the subject, the feature allows you to consider what kind of organization would best suit your piece. This is another area in which knowing your audience as well as the media outlet in which your piece will be published should influence your decision.

Three common ways of organizing your feature are chronological, conceptual, or compare and contrast. Sometimes it makes the most sense to organize your information in the order it occurred; if you were focusing on the history of collaborations between designers and athletic companies, a chronological organization would probably make the most sense.

If you want to organize your feature around key ideas or concepts, then you'd be taking a conceptual approach. For example, if you wanted to link the height of heels to the status of women, a conceptual approach might best help you develop your thesis.

As the name suggests, compare and contrast uses similarities and differences to discuss the subject. Let's say you were exploring the resurgence of Tevas and Birkenstocks. You might compare the traditional wearer of these styles to the fashion people who have jumped on the bandwagon. You could go further and talk about the differences between the standard version of these shoes and the contemporary iterations of them.

Making It Personal

Creative nonfiction is another arena in which fashion writing has been employed. Creative nonfiction refers to writing that is true – nonfiction – but uses techniques of fiction like character development, scene-setting, and dialogue. It offers flexibility and freedom while still adhering to the basic tenets of reportage. In creative nonfiction, writers can be poetic and journalistic simultaneously. Beyond memoirs like *Roots of Style: Weaving Together Life, Love, and Fashion* by designer Isabel Toledo or *Love Style Life* by street photographer and blogger Garance Doré, the use of fashion in creative nonfiction can cover the gamut of personal narrative to philosophical musing.

Love, Loss, and What I Wore Book to Stage

Sex & the City is a well-known television series and movie franchise starring Sarah Jessica Parker. What many fans don't know is that the basis for this show and the subsequent movies was an ongoing newspaper column in the '90s in *The New York Observer* by author Candace Bushnell. Bushnell has written multiple books, two of which, *Lipstick Jungle* and *The Carrie Diaries*, became popular US televisions series on NBC and the CW, respectively.

Another book that made the leap from page to stage is *Love, Loss, and What I Wore*. Written by Ilene Beckerman and published in 1995, the book is essentially a brief illustrated autobiography told through a series of different outfits. In 2008, a stage version written by Nora Ephron and her sister, Delia Ephron, premiered. Loosely based on Beckerman's book, the stage version features a variety of monologues and ensemble pieces about women, clothing, and memory. The show has been staged on six continents at last count, with its most recent production in Paris in 2012.

Kate Fletcher, one of the foremost writers on sustainable fashion, has used creative nonfiction in her exploration of sustainability and slow fashion (an issue we'll discuss in Chapter 7). In *Craft of Use: Post-Growth Fashion*, Fletcher intersperses portraits of individuals and their stories about the garments in which they are photographed, with more academic writing and exploration of fashion and sustainability. These vignettes touch on the diverse ways of thinking about the clothing that we find significant. Some of the subjects talk about the lineage of the piece and how that impacts its importance to them, others focus on the utility of a garment or the ability to move freely in it, and others discuss how an item ties them to a family member or a friend.

In *Wild Dress: Clothing & the Natural World*, Fletcher takes this thread a step further with a series of personal meditations linking garments with the natural world. These personal essays not only provide insight into Fletcher's musings on clothing and nature but also offer the reader an opportunity to know Fletcher better, which is one of the hallmarks of creative nonfiction.

In her essay, "Walking in Skirts," Fletcher discusses the utility of skirts and how she was advised by a friend in Norway to wear a silk skirt (lightweight, quick to dry) while hiking in the fjords. The skirt she wore was a modification of a '50s bias-cut silk dress that once belonged to her grandmother.

> *On the first day of the trip I put the skirt on over thick woollen leggings. It was an unusual get up, like a babushka or an onion. Layers of hand-me-down woollen jumpers, a scarf, leggings and old silk. When she saw me, Karen, the friend who I was walking with, was laughing and disbelieving. What was my motivation she wanted to know? Was I trying to get attention to flirt to pull? I insisted that the skirt was practical; practical not sexual. She raised an eyebrow. She did not know about walking in skirts. I think she took the skirt as a sign that I wasn't serious about the trip. That my mind was elsewhere. And in some ways she was right. I was the opposite of serious. I was easy and spacious and free. I was walking in a skirt.*[6]

In the past few years, there have been edited collections of essays, *Worn Stories* and *Women in Clothes*, two recent titles, which continue this theme of speaking about the self through what we wear. While these books specifically focus on the clothing and fashion, you may find that you use your knowledge of fashion in more subtle ways. For example, in writing about a relationship with a family member, you might use clothing to indicate how people are feeling or what they're thinking about. There are many ways to incorporate fashion into your writing.

The Stories We Tell

When we think of fashion and fiction, many immediately go to books that feature fashion as a central conceit such as *The Devil Wears Prada* or *Confessions of a Shopaholic*. Sometimes former fashion editors make the leap from magazine rack to bookshelf. Lucy Sykes was the fashion director of *Marie Claire* from 2001 to 2007. In 2015, she wrote (with co-author Jo Piazza) *The Knockoff*, a novel that has been said to be a combination of *The Devil Wears Prada* and the movie *All About Eve*.

But fashion in fiction doesn't have to be the main subject or at least not in the way we might think of. In *Zero History*, William Gibson writes a taut thriller that weaves together international intrigue, a cult fashion brand called Gabriel Hounds, and military-industrial contracting in a science fiction package that is still recognizable to the contemporary reader. In a scene where one of the protagonists is getting dressed, Gibson demonstrates his ability to speak convincingly about clothes as well as create an atmosphere in just a few sentences.

> *The Japanese jeans she was pulling on now, for instance. Fruit of a place around the corner from Inchmail's studio the week before. Zen emptiness, bowls with shards of pure solidified indigo, like blue black glass, the handsome older Japanese shopkeeper in her Waiting for Godot outfit.*[7]

Through the specificity of the description – the Japanese jeans, Zen emptiness, and the Samuel Beckett play *Waiting for Godot* – Gibson has created not only a mood but a very distinct visual as well. Fashion in fiction provides an opportunity to impart details about class, culture, values, and more.

Clothing in literature can be used to define characters as well as provide insight into their psychological state. One might witness a character's mental unravelling through the way their style or the care with which they dress degrades. Optimism can be implied through the colour of the protagonist's outfit, or a dark mood can be suggested by funeral garb. The passing of time can be communicated through a change in styles. As it does in real life, fashion in literature can be used to communicate more than just an aesthetic or a desire to be clothed.

The European Literature Network has recognized the role of fashion in fiction and through their Fashion and Fiction series has spoken with world-renowned writers such as Margaret Atwood, Jung Chang, Bernardine Evaristo, and Elif Shafak, who have used fashion as a central theme in many of their works. These writers, and others like them such as Chimamanda Ngozi Adichie and Salman Rushdie, don't all employ fashion in the same way, but their ability to describe and to convey meaning through fashion demonstrates the breadth of work where fashion can play a part. Fashion in literature helps propel the story forward because it helps with world building and bringing the reader from the outside in.

Child's Play

Fashion writing is not just for adults, as the journey of Serah-Marie Mahon illustrates. For many years, Mahon was best known as the editor of *Worn Fashion Journal*, an independent spirit on the fashion publication landscape. *Worn* was known for its in-depth articles on subjects such as non-binary dressing, the history of the flight attendant uniform, and the Pearly Kings and Queens of London. Mahon wanted to create a publication that wasn't focused on the commercial, mainstream idea of fashion as presented by most publications on the market. Fashion spreads in *Worn* often featured clothing borrowed from vintage stores or the models' own.

Mahon wanted the issues to be timeless, so one could pick it up at any time and find relevant content.

After ten years of publishing *Worn*, Mahon decided it was time to shut it down because the need for it had waned as other magazines entered the scene. She'd already been working as the community manager at *Type Books* in Toronto (Canada) when a discussion with Alison Matthews David, a professor at Ryerson University and the author of *Fashion Victims: The Dangers of Dress Past and Present*, led to their collaboration on a children's book based on David's research, *Killer Style: How Fashion Has Injured, Maimed, & Murdered Through History*.

One might think that although the topic is still fashion, the switch from fashion magazine editor to children's book author might be difficult. However, as Mahon explained in an interview in *Fashion*,

> At the root, it's about explaining things and getting down to "what is the juice that makes this engine turn," and then laying that out in a way that is understandable . . . I relied on my magazine publishing history really heavily while writing this kids book, in that it was about breaking down information into pieces and merging it into a theme.[8]

The skills that make one a good fashion writer have applicability across multiple genres and for multiple generations of readers.

Across the Airwaves

Podcasts have grown in popularity as a way to talk about fashion, in all its complexity. From the history-minded Dressed: The History of Fashion, to au courant conversations with designers on Creative Conversation with Suzy Menkes, to the more regionally specific discussions featured on the Dubai Fashion News podcast, there is a podcast for almost every area of interest.

If you want to start a podcast, you'll first and foremost need an idea of what you're trying to communicate. It's quite similar to approaching a piece of writing. Who is your audience for your podcast? What's the best way to communicate with them? Once you've figured out that part, create a structure for your podcast. What's the first thing that the listener hears? Do you have theme music? Does your podcast have regular features (e.g. daily fashion news or outfit of the day)? If so, when do they come in? What's the focus of each episode? How is that material communicated? If you have sponsors, when do you mention them? Do they have recorded adverts? Basically, what are the things you need to remember each time?

While the best podcasts sound like organic conversations, there is work involved in getting to that flow. There are two main approaches to writing for a podcast: the script and the show notes. The main difference is how much copy is written. The script is a fully (or almost fully) written out version of what you want to say as well as when you want to say it. A script should also include an indication of where standard features of your podcast, such as sponsor acknowledgement or information on upcoming episodes, come in.

In addition to the copy you want to read, a good script includes moments where you might pause or speak extemporaneously; i.e. just off the top of your head. These moments keep you from sounding *too scripted*, which can make a podcast feel stilted or static. If you have guests, this can be especially important because you never know how they're going to answer a question, and you want to be able to take advantage of those moments and further the conversation. Be prepared to be flexible.

A script also gives you an indication of length. How long you want your podcast to go is up to you, although most stay in the 40- to 60-minute range. You may build in moments that are either easily integrated or edited out, depending on how your conversation with your guest goes. Don't assume that the conversation will flow naturally or that you'll be able to fill in gaps in conversation. Be prepared with additional material.

If the podcast is only you, then keep your listener in mind as the other party in the discussion. While you're not waiting for an actual answer, give your listener time to consider your points.

Show notes follow more of an outline form and highlight talking points. These are generally meant to prompt your memory, and this format works well with two or more hosts because the room for dynamic conversation is built in. It also keeps you on track should the conversation veer off course. For both approaches to the podcast, you want to be sure to keep to your structure.

Putting Pen to Paper

As with any piece of writing you do, you should start with a plan. Start by thinking about the purpose of your piece. What do you want to say about your topic? You should be aware of your interest or engagement with the subject. How knowledgeable are you on it, and how much research do you think you'll have to do? Answering these questions will enable you to figure out whether you have sufficient time (research!) and interest to write this piece. It also helps to have an idea of what you hope to accomplish with it. You may find that you have to change the scope of your writing if you don't have enough time to reach your goal.

Then think about your audience, which we've discussed in some detail in Chapter 3. If you've been assigned or contracted to write the piece, you'll have a built-in audience. Who reads the media outlet in which you'll publish this piece? What do you know about them? For example, *Elle* magazine and the journal *Fashion Theory* are two very different publications, but they both might feature an article on shoes. However, their audience will expect information specific to the type of publication. For example, *Elle* magazine might feature an article on the best way to wear a certain shoe, and *Fashion Theory* could publish one on the symbolic power of the platform. Remember that readers come to expect specific things based on the publication.

Expectations can also extend to the writer; if you have published elsewhere, readers may be familiar with your work and come to expect a certain style, focus, or approach. If you're a less established writer, the readers' expectations will be focused on the publication and not you. The more you know about your audience, the better situated you are to begin writing.

Also important is to have an idea of what the readers already know about the subject. You don't want to repeat information they already have, but you also don't want to assume they're all experts either. Understanding this will enable to figure out which terms need defining and which don't. This tracks back to our discussion of writer-based prose versus reader-based prose in Chapter 3.

Your tone is the way you convey an attitude or mood about the subject. It tells the reader what you think about the subject and is communicated through your choice of words and what you decide to highlight or omit. Your tone should remain consistent with your purpose as well as with your audience. We talk a little bit more about this in Chapter 7.

Many writers find it helpful to write an outline of key points, in the order of discussion, before they begin. Others like to just start writing and then shape the work during revision, and many have a hybrid approach. With any of these approaches, you'll always write a first draft. Put all your ideas down on paper. Don't stop to edit or spellcheck. Just write. It's often easiest just to get everything down on the page, so you can see what you've got. Then you can begin the revision process. It's easier to work with what's been written than to try to pull it out of your head in the order you wish.

During the revision process, in addition to organizing your material, you can make sure that your tone and style are consistent throughout. You'll have an opportunity to emphasize important points as well as ensure that all the points you want to make are there. You can check to see that you're clear as well as ensure you're avoiding any kind of biased writing or clichés.

Once you've gotten a solid third or fourth draft done, you'll begin the editing process. Revising applies to work on the content and the shape of the piece; editing means the technical side of writing, the mechanics. How is the grammar? Are there any long and unwieldy sentences? What about spelling? Here we must stress that you should not rely on spellcheck. "There," "their," and "they're" are all correctly spelled but mean different things. These kinds of words are called homophones: they sound the same but differ in meaning and spelling. Oversights like this can undermine your authority as a writer.

A good way to catch mistakes as well as check for convoluted sentences or sentence fragments is to read your piece aloud. You don't need someone to read to, but you do need to read out loud. You'll hear awkward phrasings, wrong word choices, or strained analogies, and you'll probably do some unconscious editing as you read, such as changing a word or reordering a sentence.

Fashion Is Not Just About Fashion

Award-winning Journalist Robin Givhan Reflects on Her Career Trajectory and What It Means to Be a Fashion Journalist

As the first journalist awarded the Pulitzer Prize for criticism (2006) for their fashion coverage, Robin Givhan's ability to understand the language and power of fashion is just one of the reasons why she is admired by fashion journalists across the globe. As the senior critic-at-large for *The Washington Post*, she covers politics, race, and arts. She's interviewed not only designers and fashion industry insiders but also politicians and cultural icons, and from 2009 to 2010, she wrote about Michelle Obama and the social and cultural shifts that resulted from the first African American family in the White House.

Although her tenure at *The Washington Post*, which began in 1995, has been her longest relationship with a single outlet, her work has appeared in *Vogue*, *New York Magazine*, *The Daily Beast*, and *The Detroit Free Press*. She is also the author of *The Battle of Versailles: The Night American Fashion Stumbled Into the Spotlight and Made History*.

You distinguish your job as a journalist who covers fashion. Why do you see your role in that way?

I cover the business aspects of fashion, along with the cultural part of it, which is to say, I write about how people use fashion, how the marketing of it shapes the way we think about ourselves and other people, how the mythology surrounding fashion creates separate tribes and statuses and creates the hierarchy. I also write about it as an applied art and that it is, at its best, exquisite to look at and tells us a little bit about sort of where we are at any given moment.

In a lot of your writing, there is a sort of unpacking of things and noticing fashion, not for necessarily what it ornaments but what it communicates. What do you think the most challenging part of writing about fashion is?

I would say it's helping people understand that it's more than just colour stories and hemlines. It's no more, or less, superficial than the cinema, than digital arts, than literature, than sports – than all these other aspects of culture that we somehow inherently understand reflects something deeper, and yet there's a tendency to pigeonhole fashion as unable to do that.

There is a common misconception that fashion is anti-intellectual.

The writer Chimamanda Ngozi Adichie made a really wonderful point during an interview because after she had just gained a lot of notoriety from her books and from her TedTalk, she was offered an opportunity to participate in a marketing campaign for a cosmetics brand in the UK, and there was some criticism of that. I'm not sure if it was directly in response to the criticism or if it was just in speaking more generally, but she said that it's wrong to denigrate the pleasures of women because it is just a continuation of a form of sexism. And I think that sports is a really apt comparison because it is typically considered to be the world of men.

So we can take very seriously whether or not steroids are being used in baseball, but because fashion is perceived as the province of women, it tends to be belittled, and I think women participate in that belittling. There are women in very accomplished fields and high-powered positions, who are passionate about fashion. It delights them. It's fun. They enjoy it. And yet they are incredibly hesitant to talk about it because they feel to utter a designer's name immediately knocks down their IQ by 20 points.

You went to Princeton for your undergraduate degree. Did you study art history, or did you study English or journalism?

I was an English major at Princeton.

When you were getting your graduate degree in Journalism at the University of Michigan, were you thinking about incorporating fashion in your writing, or were you interested in another kind of journalism?

I was interested in writing and journalism in general – in reporting and writing. I wanted to be a feature writer. I had no interest in fashion, really.

What do you think is something that people might be surprised to know that they need in order to be a fashion writer?

I would say reporting skills and the ability to read an annual report. I would also say interests beyond fashion.

What are some of the issues that you think the fashion world is going to be facing in the next couple of years?

That's such a hard question. There are existential questions, and then there are practical questions. If you'd asked me this a year ago, six months ago, I probably would have said that it's understanding a sense of responsibility when it comes to diversity and inclusiveness. I think that remains something that the industry has to deal with and figure out. But more pressing than that is the industry's own business model. If [the industry] doesn't figure that out, there won't be an opportunity to think about bigger issues.

Seeing the way designers innovated around presenting shows during the pandemic, what happens to the seasons now if shows are all going online?

I remain sceptical of anything on social media, as much as I participate in it. I don't think that there is a real replacement for being able to see clothing in real life. There is something very visceral about that experience. I've always believed that a runway production may not be the best answer for every brand, but there are some brands that really take advantage of that kind of spectacle and create something that's truly memorable and dynamic. It may be that there are a dozen different answers to that question. One of which is Instagram, and one of which is the status quo. I think one of the interesting stories going forward will be to see how it unfolds and what kind of creativity designers bring to that question.

Do you think that we are moving away from the more theatrical productions of runway shows which have, over the past decades, been such an integral part of the fashion world and the collection experience?

I personally find sitting and staring at little squares (on Instagram) at a certain point to be a little bit mind-numbing, but that's my preference. Maybe it's generational. Maybe there are those who came before me who find the big theatrical productions off-putting because they're distracting, and they much prefer to see something quieter and more intimate and more meditative. When I was working on a book (*The Battle of Versailles: The Night American Fashion Stumbled Into the Spotlight and Made History*), one of the most striking things to me was a description of a Cristobal Balenciaga couture show and how the clothing was presented in complete silence.

I would find that really just sort of pretentious and overwrought, but the customers at that time, that's what they were accustomed to, and that's what they expected. So clearly a lot of it has to do with the context and the timing. I think it may also be the difference between seeing something in person and seeing it on a screen. I personally love going to see a play in a theatre, but I don't really want to watch a televised version of it.

It's a completely different experience. To me, watching a handful of actors on stage speaking some dramatic truth is really captivating. I have yet to see that same thing in the version that's been recorded for television. It's not the same thing.

Do you have a favourite piece of your own writing? One of your pieces that you love the best?

I can't really say that there's one particular piece, but the one that sort of has stayed with me was more about the experience of reporting on it, on the person. I lived in New York for about ten years, and I was there on 9/11, and so the story that I did the day after as I spent the day with a woman who was trying to get information about her relative who had worked in one of the towers – walking with her through the city, in that aftermath, and walking with her as she went from hospital to hospital. I will never forget that.

It has nothing to do with fashion obviously, but to be with someone at that moment in their life that was so personal and at the same time, affected so many people and was so transformative. It really stays with you.

Did you have a mentor coming up?

That's the odd word to me because I'm not really quite sure what that is. I had teachers and professors who were really influential in terms of my way of thinking, whom I felt comfortable enough with and close enough to that I could talk to them about decisions that I had to make in terms of my career and my education. I think there are always people along the way whom you feel that connection to. I was lucky enough to have several incredible English teachers when I was in high school to really make me love writing and love literature, and who handed me books that weren't on the syllabus, but they just thought I would enjoy reading them.

In college I was lucky enough to have several professors, in small enough classes, that really engaged on a personal level with students.

Do you have writing influences that you can point to in your own work or writing that you enjoy reading?

I had a great professor when I was in grad school, who was a working journalist and a real advocate for his students. That was really helpful. Like probably everyone else, I read *The New Yorker*, and I'm fascinated by those long, thoughtful profiles and feature stories. I read my colleagues and am inspired by their work. I really admire Sally Jenkins, a sports columnist at *The Washington Post* who writes about sports in such a broad, thoughtful, and welcoming way. I'm a big fan of Frank Bruni at *The New York Times*, who I have known forever. I worked with him in Detroit, and he has a vocabulary and a sense of phrase that is sort of dazzling. I also read a fair amount of fiction, and then there are the classic American works that you read when you're an English major.

I took creative writing when I was at Princeton and had Joyce Carol Oates. Now, make no mistake, I was not a star student, but one of the things that she said that really stuck with me was that as a writer, the first thing that you really need to do is find your voice. At the time I didn't really know exactly what she meant, but she really encouraged writing from a place that felt organic and real. In essence she was saying, absorb other people's work and consider other people's work, but you really have to find your own way of expressing yourself and your own understanding of the topic at hand. And that's what makes for memorable strong writing.

What are you reading now?

On my nightstand, there are about ten old copies of *The New Yorker*. I have Colson Whitehead's *The Underground Railroad* and Ibram X. Kendi's *Stamped From the Beginning*. It's the definitive history of racist ideas in America. I had dug out Katherine Boo's book *Behind the Beautiful Forevers: Life, Death, and Hope in a Mumbai Undercity* because it had been on my bookshelf forever, and I hadn't had a chance to read it.

Do you generally have a longer-term editorial project on the go at the same time that you're doing of the moment news pieces?

Yes. Typically there's a longer-term piece that, as they say, I'm gathering string on and thinking about and collecting data on. Then there's usually a longer piece that I'm actively working on, doing interviews for and writing, which gets interrupted with news stories.

That must keep it very dynamic and interesting.

It's nice to have stories that are on a list (on post-its on my home computer) of things that I want to get to. Invariably some of them end up falling off the list because they are timely, and I can't get to all the timely pieces in a timely manner. It's nice to be able to keep your deadlines skills sharp but also be able to stretch out and do some things that are longer-term and be able to sit with the story for a while.

If you had to do something else, what would it be?

My backup option was that I was going to go to law school.

Notes

1. Gupta, Garim. "Meet Aditi Mayer, the Sustainability Activist Decolonising Fashion, One Instagram Post at a Time." *Vogue (India)*, 10 March 2021, www.vogue.in/fashion/content/meet-aditi-mayer-the-sustainability-activist-decolonising-fashion-one-instagram-post-at-a-time
2. Bucci, Alessandro, and Philipp Ekardt. "On the Uses and Abuses of Benjamin for Thinking about Fashion. Philipp Ekardt on 'Benjamin on Fashion.'" *Fashion Theory*, 2021. DOI: 10.1080/1362704X.2021.1872851
3. Givhan, Robin. "The Language of Margaret Thatcher's Handbags." *Daily Beast*, 26 January 2021, www.thedailybeast.com/the-language-of-margaret-thatchers-handbags?ref=author.
4. Started in Tunisia and spread to Libya, Egypt, Yemen, Syria, and Bahrain.
5. Grassroots movement among First Nations, Metis, and Inuit in Canada.
6. Fletcher, Kate. *Wild Dress: Clothing & The Natural World*. Uniform Books, 2019, p. 34.
7. Gibson, William. *Zero History*. Berkeley, 2012, p. 23.
8. Slone, Isabel. "How *Worn Journal*'s Serah-Marie Mahon Went from Fashion Magazine Editor to Writing Children's Books." *Fashion*, 15 April 2019, fashionmagazine.com/style/killer-style-book/

Works Cited

Beckerman, Ilene. *Love, Loss, and What I Wore*. Algonquin, 1995.

Boo, Katherine. *Behind the Beautiful Forevers*. Random House, 2012.

Bucci, Alessandro, and Philipp Ekardt. "On the Uses and Abuses of Benjamin for Thinking about Fashion. Philipp Ekardt on "Benjamin on Fashion"." *Fashion Theory*, 2021. DOI: 10.1080/1362704X.2021.1872851

Fletcher, Kate. *Wild Dress: Clothing & the Natural World*. Uniform Books, 2019.

Gibson, William. *Zero History*. Berkeley, 2012.

Givhan, Robin. Givhan, Robin. *The Battle of Versailles: The Night American Fashion Stumbled into the Spotlight and Made History*. First Edition. Flatiron Books, 2016.

Givhan, Robin. "The Language of Margaret Thatcher's Handbags." *Daily Beast*, 26 January 2021, www.thedailybeast.com/the-language-of-margaret-thatchers-handbags?ref=author.

Gupta, Garim. "Meet Aditi Mayer, The Sustainability Activist Decolonising Fashion, One Instagram Post at a Time." *Vogue (India)*, 10 March 2021, www.vogue.in/fashion/content/meet-aditi-mayer-the-sustainability-activist-decolonising-fashion-one-instagram-post-at-a-time

Kendi, Ibram X. *Stamped from the Beginning: The Definitive History of Racist Ideas in America*. Nation Books, 2016.

Slone, Isabel. "How *Worn Journal*'s Serah-Marie Mahon Went from Fashion Magazine Editor to Writing Children's Books." *Fashion*, 15 April 2019, fashionmagazine.com/style/killer-style-book/

Whitehead, Colson. *The Underground Railroad: A Novel*. First Edition. Doubleday, 2016.

Annotated Bibliography

Allaire, Christian. *The Power of Style: How Fashion and Beauty Are Being Used to Reclaim Cultures*. Annick Press, 2021.
 This young adult book explores the connections between fashion and history, culture, politics, and social justice. Clothing is here positioned as an important element of culture and cultural expression.

Bardey, Catherine. *Wearing Vintage*. Hachette Books, 2002.
 A guide to finding, styling, and wearing vintage clothes. Complete with coloured photographs, this book is designed for vintage enthusiasts on any budget.

Barnard, Malcolm. *Fashion Theory: An Introduction*. Routledge, 2014
 This accessible introductory text explains the major theoretical foundations of fashion studies. Providing critique and contextualization, this book explores issues ranging from fashion history to the erotics and fetishization of clothing.

Boman, Eric. *Rare Bird of Fashion: The Irreverent Iris Apfel*. Thames & Hudson, 2007.
 This book contains more than 90 photos of select pieces from Iris Apfel's wardrobe, an introduction by Harold Koda, and an essay by Iris Apfel. Photos are accompanied by captions detailing dates, designers, and full information on fabrics and accessories.

David, Alison Matthews. *Fashion Victims: The Dangers of Dress Past and Present*. Bloomsbury Publishing, 2015.
 This book chronicles the history of deadly dress, from lethal materials to clothing-centred accidents in fiction and reality. Illustrated with over 125 images, this book explores the dark side of fashion.

David, Alison Matthews, and Serah-Marie McMahon. *Killer Style: How Fashion Has Injured, Maimed, and Murdered Through History*. Owlkids, 2019.
 This book examines fatal styles and clothing, with historical examples such as the Radium Girls, the Mad Hatters highlighting historical and contemporary unsafe factory conditions. With an engaging format and accessible style, this book is designed for younger readers.

Fletcher, Kate. *Wild Dress: Clothing & The Natural World*. Uniform Books, 2019.
 This book explores the relation between clothing and nature, documenting ways to wear clothes that increase awareness of the natural world. Fletcher provides a new perspective in this series of autobiographical texts.

Fletcher, Kate, and Ingun Grimstad Klepp, editors. *Opening Up the Wardrobe: A Methods Book*. Novus Press, 2017.
 A guide to gathering information about people and their clothing, this book includes 50 methods for exploring the material content of the wardrobe. Contributions to this book come from both academic and non-academic sources.

Granata, Francesca, editor. *Fashion Criticism: An Anthology*. Bloomsbury Publishing, 2021.
 This anthology explores the history of fashion criticism in English, exploring gender issues, shifts in media coverage, and changing understandings of race. The first anthology of its kind, this book covers fashion criticism in genres from early 20th-century magazines to Pulitzer Prize–winning criticism.

Heti, Sheila, Heidi Julavits, and Leanne Shapton. *Women in Clothes*. Penguin, 2014.
 A conversation between women that began as a survey about the influence of clothing on our daily lives. Six hundred and thirty-nine women here speak about the motives behind their clothing.

Mair, Carolyn. *The Psychology of Fashion*. Routledge, 2018.
: This book examines fashion in relation to psychology, exploring issues from how fashion can impact body image to the psychological manipulations of retail environments. This book asserts that psychology can inform more sustainable approaches to fashion production and consumption.

McMahon, Serah-Marie. *The Worn Archive: A Fashion Journal About the Art, Ideas & History of What We Wear*. Drawn & Quarterly Publications, 2014.
: A collection of the best content from the first 14 years of *Worn Fashion Journal*, including photos and articles on a wide range of topics relating to fashion. *Worn* is a Canadian fashion journal that investigates the relationships between fashion, pop culture, and art.

McNeil, Peter, et al., editors. *Fashion in Fiction: Text and Clothing in Literature, Film and Television*. Berg, 2009.
: A collection of essays from North American, European, and Australian theorists that explore the function of clothing within fictional narrative. This book covers a range of genres and media, from novels to advertising, exploring the ways that clothing shapes meaning.

McRobbie, Angela. *British Fashion Design: Rag Trade or Image Industry?* Routledge, 2003.
: Writing from a cultural studies perspective, Angela McRobbie explores the tensions between fashion as both an art form and a commercial industry through interviews with and research on graduate designers. This book details the processes and strategies of British graduate designers as they enter the fashion industry.

Spivack, Emily. *Worn Stories*. Chronicle Books, 2014.
: A collection of stories about items of clothing from prominent cultural figures and storytellers that reflect on the importance of clothing in the stories of our lives. Over 60 stories span the ordinary to the extraordinary, the tragic to the celebratory.

Steele, Valerie, editor. *The Berg Companion to Fashion*. Bloomsbury Publishing, 2015.
: A reference anthology that covers a wide range of topics, including the meanings, histories, and theories of fashion. Over 300 entries cover designers, clothing articles, concepts, and styles.

Steele, Valerie, editor. *Fashion Designers A–Z*. Taschen, 2020.
: A collection of photographs, illustrations, and texts written by museum curators, this book explores the importance of the fashion exhibition. This book covers a century of fashion collected in New York's Museum at the Fashion Institute of Technology.

Steele, Valerie, editor-in-chief. *Fashion Theory*. Taylor & Francis, ongoing (journal), www.tandfonline.com/action/journalInformation?show=editorialBoard&journalCode=rfft20.
: This journal publishes research about fashion as a facet of embodied identity and the cultural significance of style and clothing. Topics range beyond clothing to body modification such as piercing and tattooing.

Welters, Linda, and Abby Lillethun. *The Fashion Reader*. Berg, 2011.
: An edited collection of 76 essays and articles that aims to bring together new and established ideas in order to provide a foundation for study of the history, business, and culture of fashion. Essays are drawn from books, magazines, exhibition catalogues, and journals.

Section 3
Broadening Your Focus

Introduction

In this section, we want to familiarize you with the ways fashion can be used in writing beyond the most familiar types of fashion writing, i.e. the runway report, the service piece, and the trend report, as well as help you understand some of the current issues and trends within the fashion industry. We discuss the opportunities afforded by longer form pieces like the feature and offer a glimpse into the ways fashion has made an appearance in fiction and nonfiction. Our discussion of contemporary issues in fashion will help you see fashion in a broader context and ultimately strengthen your writing overall.

Finally, we help you pitch your first piece with detailed instruction and sample pitch letters.

7 Taking It All In
Contemporary Issues in Fashion

By this point, if you've been working through the book from the beginning, you should have a better sense of the breadth of fashion writing and many of the elements that contribute to it. This chapter will leave you with a few more things to consider before you head on your way to write compellingly about fashion.

As we've repeated throughout this book, fashion exists within a larger context, and like fashion itself, this landscape is ever-changing. As society-at-large grapples with important issues, those issues are frequently taken up by the fashion world and are not only potentially manifest on the runway but also in the programmatic focus of governing bodies and fashion-based non-profits. In fact many non-profit organizations and charities have arisen out of the need for fashion to address specific concerns. Waste and Resources Action Plan (WRAP) is one such group that focuses on sustainability issues that started as a non-profit and has since become a registered charity in the United Kingdom.

It should not be surprising that fashion would take up contemporary social and cultural issue because fashion, as we've discussed, is in conversation with the zeitgeist. In order to maintain its relevance, it needs to address the important issues of the day.

#MeToo

The phrase "me too" made its first appearance in 2006 on MySpace. Activist and sexual harassment survivor Tarana Burke coined the phrase to allow other women who'd suffered sexual harassment or assault to find solidarity together and feel empowered.

It was in 2017, when allegations against US movie producer Harvey Weinstein began to dominate the news, that the phrase and subsequent movement shot into the limelight. By 2018, the movement had gone global as women found strength in sharing their stories. #MeToo has been translated (either literally or figuratively) into many languages. In France, it's #BalanceTonPorc ("squeal on your pig"); in Arabic-speaking countries, it's #AnaKaman ("me too"); and in Italy, it's #QuellaVoltaChe ("that time when").

DOI: 10.4324/9781003047629-11

> In 2018, the Nobel Peace Prize was jointly awarded to human rights activist and Yazidi assault survivor Nadia Murad and Congolese physician Denis Mukwege "for their efforts to end the use of sexual violence as a weapon of war and armed conflict,"[1] taking the #MeToo movement to another level of discourse.

A good writer will be cognizant of these issues and be able to address them, either explicitly or implicitly, in their work. Failure to acknowledge, for example, the potential harm or good the utilization of African fashions by a non-African designer will signal to your reader that you are unaware of the discussion around cultural appropriation. Understanding some of the key issues with which fashion has been occupied will help you avoid unintended mistakes or offences.

These are by no means the only issues fashion is dealing with, but they represent some of the larger, persistent matters at hand. In this chapter, we will provide an overview of the concept of cultural appropriation, the campaign for greater diversity, and efforts in sustainability in the fashion community. We cannot answer all the questions these issues raise; however, we can provide you with a solid basic understanding of them from which you can build.

Oh. Is That Yours?

The contemporary discussion around cultural appropriation finds its roots in Edward Said's 1978 book *Orientalism*, which we touch on in Chapter 1. The *Oxford English Dictionary* defines "cultural appropriation" as "the unacknowledged or inappropriate adoption of the practices, customs, or aesthetics of one social or ethnic group by members of another (typically dominant) community or society." Designers have long looked to the aesthetics of other communities, and this is an area where fashion can get into trouble. Returning to our fashion history, we see that Paul Poirot was an unabashed borrower of styles of dress and decoration from Middle Eastern countries, which would most likely raise questions of cultural appropriation today.

As with many issues, there is more than one way to look at this. I had a conversation with a designer of Dutch and African descent about wearing African wax cloth. He was happy for women to wear it regardless of their ethnic identity. Among his designs, he himself had borrowed from Japanese culture through kimono-style sleeves and from South America via a poncho. For many designers, reinterpreting or being inspired by such design elements is part of the creativity of fashion, and their inclusion of these is seen as both an appreciation and a new expression of them. This is one reason why the discussion of cultural appropriation versus appreciation is complicated.

In recent years, designers such as Jean Paul Gaultier, John Galliano, Isabel Marant, and the house of Gucci have all been critiqued for cultural appropriation in their designs. The brand Victoria's Secret has a long list of offences, the most recent one being from their 2017 annual runway show when their looks featured elements specific to Native American culture, such as the war bonnet. Each of these brands used elements from cultures not their own, often wholesale, in their designs. The lack of any acknowledgement as well as the extravagant price tag associated with the designer items (when many of the original influences are predominantly worn or created by people of modest means) added an additional layer of outrage.

The global ramifications of cultural appropriation have not gone unnoticed. The United Nations has been compelled to establish protections for Indigenous peoples worldwide. Article 11 of the United Nations Declaration of the Rights of Indigenous Peoples speaks to the threat that cultural appropriation poses to these communities and states that they have the right not only to practise their cultural traditions but also to "maintain, protect, and develop the past, present and future manifestations of their cultures, such as . . . artefacts, designs . . . and visual and performing arts and ceremonies." They go further to speak of the possibility of Indigenous cultures receiving compensation for cultural property that is taken without consent. It is important to understand that cultural appropriation can go beyond simply "borrowing" another culture's creative expression without permission; it can undermine their identity.

Appreciation Versus Appropriation

One of the challenges in discussing cultural appropriation is that there isn't always a clear distinction between appropriating and *appreciating* a culturally specific element. Fashion editors have felt compelled to explicate the difference to their readers as demonstrated by an article *TeenVogue* published in 2016 where they asked seven young women to talk about their culturally specific beauty looks.[2] For some, any use of another's culture, regardless of acknowledgement, is to be avoided at all costs. For others, the question of what constitutes appropriate acknowledgement, and whether that includes financial compensation, is at the forefront of their thoughts on the matter.

In 2021, the government of Mexico accused fashion brands Zara, Anthropologie, and Patowl of cultural appropriation through their use of design motifs and techniques specific to Indigenous Mexican communities and sought recompense for those communities. In their press release about the open letter to these companies, they said,

> The Ministry of Culture of Mexico has addressed several letters to Zara, Anthropologie and Patowl, pronouncing itself against undue cultural appropriation and thus asking for a public explanation on what ground they have decided to privatize collective property, making use of cultural elements from Oaxacan communities, as well as the benefits that will be rewarded to the creative communities.[3]

At the time of publication, there had been no financial benefit provided by the brands to the Indigenous communities.

There is a deep history of colonialism among Western countries, which is one of the main arguments against ideas of appreciation versus appropriation. Many see any use as appropriation and simply a continuation of the legacy of colonialism. However, for others, this diminishes the possibility of not only reviving a possibly lost art or craft but also allowing others to expand in their understanding of other cultures. Connie Wang, host of the documentary series *Style Out There* and former executive editor at Refinery29, addressed this in her opinion piece for the *New York Times Sunday Review*, titled "Finding Beauty in Cultural Appropriation" (originally titled "Can Cultural Appropriation Be Beautiful?"). In it she writes,

> [R]eframing fashion-based cultural appropriation not as a bad habit but as a discussion of ideas helps make these calculations [determining whether cultural appropriation is O.K.] easier. We understand how ideas work. Sometimes they're unnecessarily offensive, and sometimes they're offensive because they need to be. Sometimes the controversy they generate is silly and piddling; other times it's enlightening. As my seatmate in Lagos told me, it can help us see something we would have otherwise missed.[4]

As demonstrated through these examples, there is no consensus on cultural appropriation. The following are some ways you can decide whether a designer is aptly "borrowing" from a culture not their own. You can start by finding out whether they have publicly acknowledged the influence and given credit to the original culture. From there, you can question whether they are employing the element in a manner that is respectful of the original culture. Does it understand the history of this borrowed element? Does this "borrowing" reinforce stereotypes or misrepresent the original culture? Finally, it is important to recognize who is appropriating from whom. Cultural appropriation is not a two-way street. Dominant cultures have helped themselves to the cultural assets of marginalized communities, more often than not fostered by colonization. When marginalized communities adopt a practice or aesthetic from a dominant group, it is not cultural appropriation. The adoption is frequently due to pressure from the dominant group to assimilate, i.e. to be more like the dominant culture and to minimize difference.

Who Is Present and Accounted For?

Another cultural issue that fashion writers need to be aware of is the topic of diversity and inclusion in the fashion industry. In the past few decades, recognition of the lack of diversity among not only models but also designers has come to the forefront. As the discussion in the public sector has grown in urgency, the lack of diversity within fashion houses, organizations, and publications has come under greater scrutiny.

> ### Nude Is Not a Colour
>
> For many years, "nude" was the term used for a shade that was somewhere between champagne and sand, essentially the skin tone of a Caucasian woman. Pantone's colour called "nude" (colour 12–0911 TPX) is

a pink-leaning beige. For years, this term has excluded anyone who wasn't white. While this has been a subject of discussion in the beauty and fashion industry for almost two decades, it is only recently that it has hit the mainstream consciousness.

Hashtags such as #notmynude, which started on Twitter in 2016, have helped raise the consciousness of many; also in 2016, then School of Visual Arts (NYC) student Anastasia Warren created a photo series of the same name featuring women of colour in make-up or clothing that was called "nude." While the fashion industry is still catching up, many designers now have a range of tones in that category, understanding that women of all skin tones participate in fashion. For most, "nude" is no longer used as the term for a specific colour.

The beauty industry caught on earlier and brought attention to this as well as helped crayon manufacturer Crayola better represent the diversity of its users. In 1949, Crayola introduced a crayon called "flesh." In 1956, the name was changed to "pink beige" and then to "peach" in 1962. In 1992, working with Victor Casale (former R&D director at MAC and current CEO of MOB Beauty), Crayola developed the Colors of the World crayon collection, featuring 24 different colours to reflect the global spectrum of skin tones. In 2020, Crayola was recognized by the Shorty Awards for their efforts in the Social Good Campaign category.

In general terms, commitments to diversity seek to increase representation of individuals of different ethnicities or races, body shapes, gender expression, age, and abilities. It is understood that people of differing sizes, ages, abilities, and ethnicities engage with fashion. The exclusion of them within the business end of fashion has not only hindered the world of fashion itself but has also helped to perpetuate stereotypes and marginalized these groups. In regards to Black, Indigenous, People of Colour (BIPOC) designers, this also translates to coverage by the press and is frequently manifest through who gets celebrated and who doesn't.

The acknowledgement of the legacy of racism felt around the globe in recent years has pushed the need for increased Black representation in fashion. In January 2019, the Council of Fashion Designers of America (CFDA) released their brief on diversity and inclusion in American fashion. "The goal of the briefing is to bring awareness and start the education around all aspects of diversity and inclusion including but not limited to, abilities, age, gender, race/ethnicity, and sexual orientation." In June 2020, The Kelly Initiative – a group of Black fashion professionals – sent a letter to the CFDA outlining their plan to create tangible results in light of what they felt was the CFDA's allowance of "exploitative cultures of prejudice, tokenism, and employment discrimination to thrive."

The British Fashion Council (BFC) released their Diversity, Equity and Inclusion Policy in May 2021. Later that year, in conjunction with the BBC, they launched 50:50 The Equality Project "as a voluntary monitoring system, with the target of creating content that fairly represents the audiences it serves." Starting with London Fashion Week in September 2021, they began collecting data on the diversity of not only models and design teams but hair, makeup, and all other teams involved in production as well.

This is an ongoing issue, and as demonstrated by the sidebar on *Vogue* covers featuring diverse models, it is a long overdue one. As you report on the fashion industry and cover runways, look for how inclusion issues are being addressed. More and more designers are using more diverse models on the runway. In addition to increasing racial diversity, fashion houses have recently welcomed more plus-size models to their runways. Fendi, Chanel (once under fire for anti-fat comments made by Karl Lagerfeld), and Alexander McQueen all featured plus-size models in their AW2020 shows.

Watershed Moments for Diversity in *Vogue*

- March 1966 – Donyale Luna is the first Black model on the cover of *Vogue UK*.
- August 1974 – Beverly Johnson is the first Black model on the cover of *Vogue US*.
- August 1988 – Naomi Campbell is the first Black model on the cover of *Vogue Paris*.
- September 2018 – Disabled models (Jillian Mercado, Mama Cax, and Chelsea Werner) are featured on individual covers of *TeenVogue*.
- August/September 2021 – Environmentalist Greta Thunberg, who has been open about her Asperger's, is on the cover of the inaugural issue of *Vogue Scandinavia*, which also features the first fashion editor who wears a hijab (Rawdah Mohamed).
- September 2021 – An ensemble of diverse models features the first Asian plus-size model (Yumi Nu) as well as the first transgender model on the cover of Vogue US (Ariel Nicholson).

Ageism is also being tackled. As a Black woman, just under 5-foot-5, JoAni Johnson managed to overcome a number of biases in fashion when she *began* modelling at age 65. Her career took off when she was featured in a video collaboration between *Allure* magazine and StyleLikeU, a mother-daughter enterprise committed to encouraging diversity, inclusion, and radical self-love in the fashion industry. In the video, part of the Dispelling Beauty Myths series, Johnson speaks about how she learned to love her grey hair. The video went viral, and Johnson's life changed. She has walked the runway for Ozwald Boateng and has been featured in advertisements for Pyer Moss. In 2020, Rihanna picked Johnson to appear in beauty campaigns for her brand Fenty. With over 75,000 followers on Instagram, she shows no sign of slowing down.

In 2017, at age 85, Carmen Dell'Orifice was chosen to close Guo Pei's couture show as part of Paris Couture Week. Dell'Orifice began her modelling career at the age of 15, when she was photographed by Cecil Beaton for *Vogue* magazine. Still actively modelling, Dell'Orifice turned 90 in June 2021. Another example of endurance in the modelling industry is Daphne Selfe. A recipient of a British Empire Award, Selfe is still going strong as a model in her 90s. While she began modelling in 1949, she left the industry when she married and began a family. It wasn't until she was cast in a Red or Dead runway show at 70 years of age that her career actually took off. Since then, she has worked with Dolce & Gabbana, British *Vogue*, and others. The careers of Johnson, Dell'Orifice, and Selfe are an indication that the fashion industry is beginning to understand that not only do older women still care about fashion, but they also want to see themselves reflected in the pages of magazines and on the runway.

We have only touched upon the issue of diversity here, but having an awareness of this topic and actively looking for it can positively inform your next piece of fashion journalism. A fashion writer should see the big picture. Understanding the power fashion has over individuals through representation – to celebrate them, to validate their participation in fashion, and to inspire – underscores fashion's influence on culture at large.

How Long Can This Go On?

The final area we'll discuss is sustainability, an issue, like cultural appropriation and diversity, that has global repercussions. In Chapter 5 we used sustainability as an example of a maxitrend, meaning that it has been an area of concern for anywhere between 10 and 30 years. It has three main areas of focus: textiles, workers, and the environment. Once again, being aware of and up-to-date on an issue such as sustainability marks you as a writer who is seeing the world of fashion within a larger context and positions you to make thought-provoking connections and write engrossing copy.

In 2018, it was discovered that the upmarket fashion label Burberry had, over the previous five years, destroyed more than £90 million worth of merchandise in an effort to protect its brand by eliminating the possibility of past season's products reaching the marketplace. The magnitude of this shocked many who had hitherto been unaware of the waste and environmental damage inflicted by the fashion industry.

Five years previously, the devasting Dhaka garment factory collapse (also known as the Rana Plaza collapse) claimed the lives of 1134 factory workers in Bangladesh. Brands such as Prada, Joe Fresh, Mango, and Primark all had garments manufactured there. This disaster brought attention to the conditions under which mass-produced fashion often takes place. While many such factories, also known as sweatshops, are located in Asia and Central and South America, they also exist in the United Kingdom, the United States, and other such countries.

> ### Fashion Revolution
>
> Fashion Revolution is one of the many organizations that has been working to transform the fashion industry through the adoption of practices that foster sustainability. Founded after the 2013 Rana Plaza building collapse, Fashion Revolution is focused on creating change through global action. Their vision is to see "[a] global fashion industry that conserves and restores the environment and values people over growth." Each year they sponsor Fashion Revolution week, which coincides with the anniversary of the Rana Plaza disaster (April 24). During the week, they encourage people to consider the factory workers who made their clothing. Participants upload images of themselves on social media, with the hashtag #whomademyclothes? to demonstrate their investment in these issues to manufacturers and to challenge them to adopt practices that protect the environment and the workers. Those who work in factories are encouraged to post their own images with the hashtag #imadeyourclothes. Fashion Revolution provides resources for not only individuals but also brands, retailers, manufacturers, and other looking to get involved with changing the fashion industry landscape.

Many of the brands manufacturing at Rana Plaza are what are considered fast fashion brands. Fast fashion brands offer affordable alternatives to high-end designer merchandise. Frequently accused of breaking copyright laws through their copies of such merchandise, fast fashion takes the looks from the runway and produces cheaper versions. Not tied to the cycle of the fashion calendar, they often produce 52 new collections a year, essentially one a week, in order to keep consumer interest high. This has a great impact on workers and the environment as the speed with which garments need to be produced offers little room for workers' rights or environmentally sound practices.

Slow fashion is an informal movement that offers resistance to the intensity of fast fashion. By taking a more considered approach to fashion, and valuing characteristics such as the durability and sustainability of textiles, slow fashion adherents hope to lessen the environmental impact of fashion as well as the negative impact on workers by buying less, mending worn clothing, and recycling their clothing whether through refashioning it, swapping it, or repurposing it.

There are a number of initiatives on sustainability in fashion. The United Nations Alliance for Sustainable Fashion works with other UN bodies to achieve targets set by the Sustainable Development Goals blueprint, which is a large-scale effort to achieve global justice through addressing sustainability and other widespread challenges. These goals address issues of workers' rights, such as pay and working conditions, and the environment, such as reducing the amount of waste produced by the fashion industry as well as the pollution caused by production.

In the United Kingdom, the BFC established the Positive Fashion Initiative, which focuses on the environment, people, and community and craftmanship.

The CFDA Guide to Sustainable Strategies provides resources for those looking to develop more sustainable practices, and in Canada, "Fashion Takes Action is a non-profit organization established in 2007 to advance sustainability in the fashion industry through education, awareness, research and collaboration."[5]

It's all well and good to talk about, but how does it show up on the runways or on the shelves? Going back to our example of the trend pyramid in Chapter 5, we spoke about the use of mushroom leather. Seeking alternatives to high-impact materials is one way designers address sustainability. In addition to alternatives to leather, designers are looking for ways to recycle materials.

Organizing Bodies in Fashion

The CFDA and the BFC are just two organizations that focus on the fashion industry and/or designers in their home countries. Often these bodies help coordinate fashion weeks, provide resources to their members, and generally work to increase the global presence of their designers. Here are just a few other such organizations:

- The Fédération de la Haute Couture et de la Mode in France (FHCM), which has three central bodies: haute couture, women's ready-to-wear, and men's ready-to-wear
- The German Fashion Designers Foundation (GFDF)
- The Fashion Designers Association of Nigeria (FADAN)
- Hong Kong Fashion Designers Association (HKFDA)
- United Fashion is an organization receiving support from the Creative Europe programme of the European Union and brings together a number of Europe-based fashion associations under one umbrella

On-demand manufacturing, the production of only the garments ordered rather than a full inventory of all available styles that season, is another example of these kinds of initiatives. For many small designers, this has been the way they have survived during the pandemic. It makes good business sense, and it lessens the impact on the environment.

Fashion brands and designers have also started providing information about the supply chain for garments. While outdoor lifestyle brands such as Patagonia adopted manufacturing transparency years ago, this is relatively new in the fashion world. Fashion brands such as the London-based Sheep Inc. and the Italian luxury goods producer Loro Piana provide production chain information, right down to the sheep. Everlane, a US-based label, supplies detailed information on the factories that produce their goods. More and more fashion labels are understanding that many consumers want their goods to reflect their values.

Putting Pen to Paper

How does this impact your writing specifically?

Just as people are valuing diversity and inclusion in the fashion industry, your writing should also be inclusive and unbiased. Not only will this kind of writing be more persuasive should you be making an argument, but it can also help dismantle stereotypes. We have already spoken about understanding who your audience is, and if you're writing for a publication that reaches an international audience, you'll want to be sure that it respects them all equally. Be aware of commonly held values or social mores among the audience.

One of the first things that will make this easier is using a shared vocabulary, which was discussed in Chapter 3. Strive to use accessible language, and avoid culturally specific idiomatic language. No one wants to feel like they're left out of the discussion.

Writing Without Bias (and How to Check for It)

We sometimes unintentionally cause offence. There's a learning curve here and sometimes along the way we can communicate unconscious bias. The best thing is to be aware of it and then correct and acknowledge your mistake, revise your copy, and move forward as a better educated writer. In recent years, cancel culture (also known as call-out culture) has been used as a blunt instrument to rectify offensive speech, writing, and actions. As a fashion writer, you have the opportunity to help move the conversation forward by helping others understand and work through elements they may not have considered.

There are a number of ways to check if your language is biased or insensitive. First, does your word choice betray a positive or negative spin? For example, many people feel strongly about mushrooms: they often either love or hate them. If you were someone who loved mushrooms, you might describe their flavour as meaty or as having an earthy taste. If, however, you hate mushrooms, you might say they taste like dirt. Both might be technically correct, but one indicates a preference while the other indicates a disdain.

When providing details, investigate whether any unnecessary information has been provided, which might colour the interpretation. For example, if you are providing information about a designer's race or gender, interrogate whether that is important for what you are trying to communicate to your audience. If you note that a designer is Chinese, for instance, are you suggesting that this is unusual or indicates a specific approach or aesthetic? If the designer does employ culturally specific elements, this might address questions of cultural appropriation; however, if it is not related to their design aesthetic or another relevant aspect of their work, then ask yourself why you've included it.

Be specific. If it is important to include race, use the name of the nation or region of origin. Avoid generalized origins like Asian, Latin American, or European. Terms like Chinese, Chilean, or German are far more specific and appropriate, and they demonstrate a level of attention in your writing. The same is true of terms specific to gender identity, sexual orientation, or disability. Use gender-neutral terms. Avoid "man" as a term for all human beings; more inclusive terms include "individuals," "people," or "persons," and use gender-neutral pronouns, such as "they/their" rather than "he/him," when speaking of mixed-sex groups. If you are unsure of the correct term, ask either the subject or someone who is well-versed in this area.

In general, you want to avoid terminology that reinforces stereotypes around gender, race, age, ability, class, or sexual orientation. When using specific descriptors, use them as adjectives and not labels (e.g. "elderly people" [adjective] versus "the elderly" [label]). Take the time to look through your writing carefully. By doing so, you'll help establish your credibility as a writer and reach a broader audience.

Fashion writing is about so much more than clothes. By being aware of the world at large and the issue that demands our attention, you should be able to write with confidence.

Future Fashion

Journalist and Sustainability Activist Bandana Tewari Talks About How She Went From Film School to the Pages of Vogue India *to Being a Leading Sustainability Activist in Fashion*

Growing up in northeast India, Bandana Tewari never set out to live a life in fashion. With a passion for filmmaking, she set her sights on becoming a documentary filmmaker, but before she could fully actualize that pursuit, fashion came calling.

In addition to being the fashion features director of *Vogue India* for 13 years, Tewari's publishing credits include *Elle India* and *The Business of Fashion*. In 2006, she was named fashion journalist of the year at the Fashion Awards in Mumbai.

What brought you to fashion in the first place?

It was most convoluted because I didn't study fashion journalism. I didn't even study journalism. I did my Master's in filmmaking, and I studied global cinema. It was the most intense four years of my life. We studied Fellini and Russian cinema and South American cinema. It was incredible. And it wasn't about fashion at all. It was a small group, and we were obsessed. All I did was wear baggy T-shirts, no makeup, no blow-outs – the antithesis of *Vogue*. Of course, we had to write scripts, and then the visualization. So, storytelling was a big part of it.

After my films studies, I joined the Discovery Channel. I wanted to be a documentary filmmaker, and the network had just arrived in India. No one was going to give me an assistant camera job; I had to earn my chops. But I was so bored in the role that I did have that I would read scripts from the Discovery Channel archives. That's when I found a series of documentaries on fashion that were done in the seventies, and the scripts were phenomenal. The topics were fashion and sexuality, fashion and politics, fashion and the economy – all beautifully done. Essentially I taught myself fashion history.

When did you start writing about fashion?

I just started dabbling in a little bit. I would write 500 words for the *Times of India* newspaper, which is the largest selling English daily in the world. I had this tiny, little column at the back with all the dirty ads, but I didn't care. I think I got $20 for the articles, but I just put my head down, and I kept writing and kept writing. And because I don't come from a fashion background, I used the lens of all of my education in sociology, psychology, filmmaking, art, and literature to see fashion through. That was interesting to me, the context of fashion.

Did you ever cover the trends?

Of course. What's the trend for the season? But I would always think, what is this fascination about black? From Japanese culture to the Parisians, to New York, all of that, just deep diving. It's so profound and deep, and it spans centuries. The monarchies and Indigenous cultures and the dying cultures . . . In India, for instance, there wasn't even the term "black"; you had indigo, and you would do the deepest, deepest indigo dyes. And that itself was called "black."

How did you move from the newspaper into magazines?

Well, writing these $20 articles for a long time built my body of work, and at that time, *Elle India* was the only top fashion magazine in the country. The editor was an amazing woman, Nonita Kalra, who eventually became my friend, and at one point, she just gave me two pages in the magazine to write what I wanted to write.

The context of India at the time was that Western fashion was a very new thing. This is the time when Louis Vuitton and Gucci were opening shops, and there was a whole buzz because India's GDP was rising. People were consuming and saying that we were on our way to being extremely affluent. But I was writing about fashion androgyny, fashion and gender . . . I don't think I even used the word "diversity" because it wasn't defined that way at the time, but that's exactly what I did. I wrote about the LGBT community. I wrote about trans fashion.

By the time *Vogue* came, the market opened up for luxury. That was my first full-time job.

At Vogue?

Yes. I was freelancing with *Elle*, and I decided I never wanted to sit in an office, but when *Vogue* comes calling . . .

Did your writing storytelling change at that point?

Initially, there was a pride that there was going to be a *Vogue India*. Even though we are a 5,000 year-old civilization, it was like saying "We have arrived" because we have validation from the Western eye. I was the fashion features director and in charge of all storytelling at the magazine (and it was published in English), so the stories needed to be accessible to a number of countries all over the world. For me, I thought this is the time to showcase India.

We did fabulous stories – the culture of India, the little black sari. If something was good overseas, we had something to talk about in this country.

Was there any story that really has stayed with you?

Yes. There's a wonderful academic who had done a coffee table book on Indian jewellery. Every time we were shooting jewellery, it was very much a Western paradigm of what is erogenous, from the Western lens. But if you look at the culture of jewellery in India, the erogenous zones are the nape of your neck, your hair, the belly, the forehead. So we did this beautiful shoot in Goa with two gorgeous brown women where they looked like Kamasutra girls basically, but only focusing on these new erogenous zones.

When you start thinking cinematically, everything matters, everything you look at is about planning the story – what's in the foreground and background, even metaphorically as a writer, that's where the context comes in. So I can talk about the thing that's in the foreground and what's happening in the background. What's the culture of that place? What's the politics of that place when women started making the sari sexy in India? What did it mean that these women were getting more emancipated? They were getting more free with their sexuality. Very much like the Diane Von Furstenberg wrap dress.

That dress came out in the '70s, when the pill became very popular with women, and they were wearing wrap dresses because you could take it off, fornicate, and put it back on, in your heels. She was so popular she was on the cover of *Time* magazine, and it was because of the sexual revolution. That context is what really makes me want to be in this business.

In fashion, there has historically been a culture of excess. What has been your experience with it, and how do you feel it impacts the conversation of sustainability?

At *Vogue* we were inundated with stuff. I had so much stuff I didn't have to buy anything. And I lived in a massive house in Bombay. I was in Paris three times a year, two times or three times in Milan and New York and Berlin. When I think about it, I can talk about it freely now, but what saved me was that I was fundamentally just a writer. Literally me, my computer, and my words.

What type of writing have you done the most of? And how do you feel it helped you evolve as a writer?

My main job [at *Vogue*] was to go and meet the designers and interview them one-on-one, no barrier, no PR barricade, no marketing barricade. I got to fly to a place, sit face-to-face, and interview these incredible people in the creative world. It was a great opportunity for me to be a storyteller and not ask the same questions as everyone else, "What is your inspiration for the season?" Even designers hate that.

I had an incredible interview with Karl Lagerfeld. And Karl Lagerfeld does not wanna be interviewed by you. He doesn't care. But when he's ready, they call you. So I get a call to fly to Paris to interview Karl Lagerfeld. And I am a geek, and there is nothing I don't know about him – every collection, his background, foreground, everything. There I am in Paris sitting next to him, and he's got his typical black sunglasses on, and so I start. "In 1962 you did this whole collection on the streets of New York, where you put models on the street, wearing ballerina flats and your dresses with leather jackets." And he says, "Passe. What is over is over. I don't talk about that."

Well, there went half my questions. So I jumped to his upcoming collection, and he told me that in his mind, it was already over. So now, 100 per cent of my questions are out. At that point, I realize I just have to rely on myself so I look at him and say, "Let's talk about your mother."

He pulled his sunglasses down, and I thought he was gonna slap me. And he says, "You know, Bandana, my mother always told me my head was too big for my body." And that broke the ice. We talked about his mother, his childhood, that he was such a geek. He was reading books when he was 10-years old, that university kids were reading, and we did not talk about clothes. We didn't talk about clothes, but we could see the genius in him because of all of these influences in his life.

You came into fashion at a time when fashion media were demigods and lavished with gifts and parties and access. Do you think that the excess of those years informed and impacted the stories you began to tell about sustainability?

Absolutely. You feel heavy with the stuff, the direction of fashion which is just more and more. And the fashion media is telling consumers that they are only valid when they have the Hermès bag, when they are wearing that watch . . . and I was the person writing those stories.

I was lucky in a way to be part of the most excessive time in fashion. I'm talking about flying to the best of cities in the world, staying in the best hotels. One day I am in Sicily meeting with Dolce and Gabbana, and then I'm in Tokyo with Raf Simmons. But it was also a time when we started to dismiss storytelling, and words were not valued, and I'm living in India, with poverty in front of you and a billionaire on your right.

So I started reaching my tipping point and feeling unhappy, and my daughter and I just packed up and left. I gave away 90% of my things and came to Bali with three suitcases.

How did sustainability become a focus of your work?

One day I am sitting on a flight, and I start thinking about Gandhi's principles and how we can apply them to the fashion industry. During this time when we were starting to talk about hyper-consumerism and operating with a centralized fashion system that controls the regions that have nothing to do with Paris, and yet Parisians are telling us what fashion should be in cultures where colour is everything.

So I started writing this speech. I didn't even know where I was gonna give it, but I wrote the whole Gandhi speech. I had, over the years become good friends with [fashion writer] Suzy Menkes, and coincidentally, at the same time, Suzy sends me a letter asking me if I would do the keynote speech at the Condé Nast International Luxury Conference in Oman in 2017.

She'd heard me in Copenhagen at a fashion summit speaking on a panel, and it resonated with her. We'd spent a lot of time together, but I didn't think she would ask me to be a keynote speaker at the best luxury conference in the world. Everyone from Jonathan Newhouse [CEO of Condé Nast] to Alber Elbaz, the designer of Lanvin, was there. Suzy gave me that opportunity, and it went off beautifully.

Everyone, including Newhouse had a Gandhi story. I just did not expect that kind of response. And that changed my life. I took that speech all over the world to Sydney, to Berlin, into Jakarta, to Bombay, and it changed my editorial pattern. I found my purpose in sustainability, mindfulness, conscious consumption. All of that became very much part of my life purpose.

Do you feel like the industry is ready for that change?

If you look at the new editors who have now arrived in all the continental publications, (all the ones who were in the front row with me are gone) the takeover is by younger people who grew up in the world of the climate crisis. They have internalized sustainability as not just a trend; they're living it.

Are the designers also ready?

Oh, there's a lot of greenwashing. The designers are in a bit of a conundrum because they've already started these businesses, which have the supply chain and the whole cycle of production established. Sustainability wasn't part of the agenda. And I do feel sorry, especially for the big designers and fast fashion companies that own 200 shops in every country, like the H&Ms and Zaras. Now you have to upend that old system.

I do feel really, really optimistic about the younger designers in every country. They are the ones who are planting the seeds of sustainability from the inception of the brand.

No one can be a hundred percent sustainable. Even the founder of Patagonia will tell you this. It opened my eyes that we do have a carbon footprint, no matter what we do as human beings. But these smaller designers (when I say small it's what I advocate now because bigger is not better) are making a mark. And we have similar ethics about what we think about the environment, human beings, humanity, what have you. They are also great storytellers because they grew up in the world of Instagram and Facebook, and so they are the ones who are engineering behind-the-scenes stories in the most prolific ways.

Do you think that the impact of telling the stories and pulling back the curtain of sustainability and contemporary social and environmental issues is actually moving the fashion industry along?

We haven't made great strides, but the storytelling is very much part of the mind shift for consumers. There was a time when product was king. It was just the product, the product, the product, the product. But now, because of this new type of storytelling, we highlight the process, the people. And now that's the purpose.

Notes

1. The Nobel Peace Prize 2018. NobelPrize.org. *Nobel Media AB 2021*, 18 March 2021. www.nobelprize.org/prizes/peace/2018/summary/
2. Welteroth, Elaine. "7 Girls Show What Beauty Looks Like When It's Not Appropriated." *TeenVogue*, 21 April 2016, www.teenvogue.com/story/beauty-cultural-appreciation-hair-makeup.
3. "La Secretaría de Cultura pide explicación a las marcas Zara, Anthropologie y Patowl por apropiación cultural en diversos diseños textiles." 28 May 2021, www.gob.mx/cultura/prensa/la-secretaria-de-cultura-pide-explicacion-a-las-marcas-zara-anthropologie-y-patowl-por-apropiacion-cultural-en-diversos-disenos-textiles. Press release. Translated from the original Spanish by Ana Lucía Sarmiento.
4. Wang, Connie. "Finding Beauty in Cultural Appropriation?" *NYTimes Sunday Review*, 20 April 2019, www.nytimes.com/2019/04/20/opinion/cultural-appropriation-coachella.html?searchResultPosition=3.
5. Fashiontakesaction.com.

Works Cited

"La Secretaría de Cultura pide explicación a las marcas Zara, Anthropologie y Patowl por apropiación cultural en diversos diseños textiles." 28 May 2021, www.gob.mx/cultura/prensa/la-secretaria-de-cultura-pide-explicacion-a-las-marcas-zara-anthropologie-y-patowl-por-apropiacion-cultural-en-diversos-disenos-textiles. Press release. Translated from the original Spanish by Ana Lucía Sarmiento.

Wang, Connie. "Finding Beauty in Cultural Appropriation?" *NYTimes Sunday Review*, 20 April 2019, www.nytimes.com/2019/04/20/opinion/cultural-appropriation-coachella.html?searchResultPosition=3.

Welteroth, Elaine. "7 Girls Show What Beauty Looks Like When It's Not Appropriated." *TeenVogue*, 21 April 2016, www.teenvogue.com/story/beauty-cultural-appreciation-hair-makeup.

Annotated Bibliography

Abloh, Virgil, and Warsh, Larry. *Abloh-isms*. Princeton University Press, 2021.
  A book of quotations from Virgil Abloh on a range of subjects from creativity to race. Abloh was the first African American artistic director of a major fashion house, who founded the luxury streetwear brand Off-White.

Anguelov, Nikolay. *The Dirty Side of the Garment Industry: Fast Fashion and Its Negative Impact on Environment and Society*. Taylor & Francis Group, 2016.

This book examines issues of overconsumption, labour exploitation, and environmental destruction as they relate to the international fashion industry. Anguelov here provides recommendations for change along with his critique of the fashion industry.

Bruzzi, Stella, and Pamela Church Gibson, editors. *Fashion Cultures Revisited: Theories, Explorations and Analysis.* Routledge, 2013.

This second anthology examines a wide range of contemporary fashion issues, including capitalism and globalization, the making of masculinities and femininities, lesbianism, and feminism. This second edition covers the time period from the beginning of the millennium to the present.

Brydon, Anne, and Sandra Niessen, editors. *Consuming Fashion: Adorning the Transnational Body.* Berg, 1998.

This anthology collection explores issues of identity-making, power and authority, gender, sexuality, and race in relation to global fashion. Interdisciplinary, ethnographic essays link theory and practice to style and clothing across time and culture.

Cheang, Sarah, Erica De Greef, and Takagi Yoko, editors. *Rethinking Fashion Globalization.* Bloomsbury Visual Arts, 2021.

This edited volume is comprised of critical scholarship on Eurocentric dominance within fashion histories. Chapters are divided into themes of Disruption in Time and Space, Nationalism and Transnationalism, and Global Design Practices and aim to complicate and remap fashion origins.

Cline, Elizabeth L. *Overdressed: The Shockingly High Cost of Cheap Fashion.* Portfolio, 2013.

This book explores the environmental, economic, and social cost of cheap fashion. Cline examines the social and economic factors that sustain fast fashion.

Eicher, Joanne B. *Berg Encyclopedia of World Dress and Fashion.* Berg, 2010.

This book contains broad overview articles about the global fashion industry, its cultural and environmental impacts, as well as a range of fashion topics from cosplay to online avatars. Taking a cross-cultural, multidisciplinary approach, this book is suitable for scholars and practitioners of fashion across disciplines.

Eluwawalage, Damayanthie, editor. *Fashion: Tyranny and Revelation.* Inter-Disciplinary Press, 2016.

This edited volume draws together socioeconomic and philosophical theories on fashion in society. Chapters explore the meanings of individual and collective clothing choices within society, highlighting fashion's function as a signifier power and status.

Fletcher, Kate. *Craft of Use: Post-Growth Fashion.* Routledge, 2016.

Focusing on sustainability in fashion, this book positions garment design and use beyond continuous consumption, as lived processes rather than static products. Attending to the use, wear, and creation of garments, Fletcher offers a diversified view of fashion beyond the market.

Fletcher, Kate. *Sustainable Fashion and Textiles: Design Journeys.* Routledge, 2012.

This book aims to provide innovative ways of thinking about the value of sustainability in garments and textiles through an exploration of the life cycle of a garment and design approaches for a sustainable future. This second edition includes a new preface, conclusion, and updated content.

Fletcher, Kate, and Lynda Grose. *Fashion and Sustainability: Design for Change.* Laurence King, 2012.

This book examines the ways in which sustainability can transform fashion products, systems, and design practices to bring about systematic change. Fletcher focuses on three types of transformations within the industry: those that occur over the life cycle of a garment, those that could transform the fashion industry at its core, and transformations in the roles of fashion designers.

Fletcher, Kate, and Mathilda Tham, editors. *Routledge Handbook of Sustainability and Fashion*. Routledge, 2015.
Using a multidisciplinary approach, this book explores sustainability in fashion, critically analysing issues such as diversity and equity, the destructive environmental impact of the fashion industry, and female independence. Recognizing the complexity of the fashion industry, this text strives to suggest creative responses to pressing contemporary issues.

Geczy, Adam. *Fashion and Orientalism: Dress, Textiles and Culture from the 17th to the 21st Century*. A&C Black, 2013.
This book argues that the Orient is integral to the history of Western fashion and explores the extent of cross-cultural exchange and translation between East and West for the past 500 years in relation to fashion. Covering a diverse range of topics from orientalism to perfume, this book is suitable for scholars of fashion, cultural studies, and history.

Gwilt, Alison, Alice Payne, and Evelise Anicet Ruthschilling. *Global Perspectives on Sustainable Fashion*. Bloomsbury Visual Arts, 2019.
This illustrated book highlights the fashion industry's efforts to reduce its negative global impacts. Essays focusing on six global regions explore issues of sustainability, cultural, and environmental concerns.

Kaiser, Susan B., and Denise N. Green. *Fashion and Cultural Studies*. Bloomsbury Publishing, 2021.
Using a wide range of cross-cultural case studies, this book explores issues of race, ethnicity, gender, and identity in relation to fashion. This text aims to bridge theory and practice in an accessible way.

Niessen, Sandra, Ann M. Leshkowich, and Carla Jones. *Re-Orienting Fashion: The Globalization of Asian Dress*. Berg, 2003.
This book explores the globalization of Asian dress styles as a colonial, orientalist phenomenon. Researchers from a range of disciplines here destabilize the orientalist definition of fashion as an exclusively Western concept.

Parkins, Ilya, and Maryanne Dever, editors. *Fashion: New Feminist Essays*. Routledge, 2020.
This essay collection examines issues of gender, sexuality, race, age, and capitalism in relation to fashion, historically and in the present. Fashion is here taken up as a critical feminist tool by established and emerging scholars from a range of disciplines.

Reilly, Andrew, and Ben Barry. *Crossing Gender Boundaries: Fashion to Create, Disrupt and Transcend*. Intellect, 2020.
A collection of essays that examine the relationships between fashion and gender. This volume explores the ways in which fashion can both challenge and reify the gender binary, from historical and contemporary perspectives.

Tarlo, Emma. *Visibly Muslim: Fashion, Politics, Faith*. Berg, 2010.
An examination of the meanings of fashion for young British Muslim consumers and designers. Based on ethnographic research, this book aims to dispel media stereotypes about Muslim appearances.

Thompson, Henrietta, and Neal Whittington. *Remake It Clothes*. Penguin Random House, 2012.

A practical reference guide to repairing and remaking clothing that includes illustrations, essays, and step-by-step projects. This book draws together global trends, traditional practices, and modern innovations to form a comprehensive guide.

Tulloch, Carol. *The Birth of Cool: Style Narratives of the African Diaspora*. Bloomsbury Publishing, 2016.
This book considers the ways in which personal style reflects issues of racial and cultural difference, investigating the role of fashion in the creation and maintenance of Black identity, specifically, from the late 19th century to the present. This book draws on ready and homemade fashion, photos, paintings, films, and letters in its consideration of cultural difference and personal style.

Way, Elizabeth, editor. *Black Designers in American Fashion*. Bloomsbury Publishing, 2021.
This book details the hidden histories and changing contexts for Black American fashion designers and workers, exploring topics such as slavery, the civil rights movement, and segregation in relation to American fashion. New and established authors and curators employ previously unexplored sources to unearth the influence of Black designers on the American fashion industry.

8 Pitch, Please

Now that you've wrapped your head around the various types of fashion writing, as well as what makes it a genre of its own and what makes it compelling, it's time for the next step. It's time to try your hand at publishing your musings on all things fashion.

In order to publish your fashion writing, you'll need to pitch your story to a publication of your choice. This might seem like a daunting task, and quite frankly, pitching can be tricky. Pitching can feel thankless and leave you feeling dejected. Many times, you might not hear back from an editor. Sometimes, you will, with a curt form letter rejection. Other times, editors will pass on your idea but offer feedback on your pitch as well as encourage you to reach out again. And then, of course, there are the success stories, when pitches lead to publication. It's hard work, but just because something is hard, doesn't mean it's impossible.

Of course, pitching can also be highly rewarding regardless of whether or not your piece gets accepted. Pitching is a task every writer undertakes, and doing it means you're earning your way, putting in the time, and on the path to becoming a working fashion writer. Ahead, you'll find a master plan for how to pitch – outlining everything from selecting an editor to crafting a successful query.

Before we get started, here are a couple things to remember as you begin the pitching process.

- Editors can receive anywhere from 10 to 200 cold pitches daily. Sometimes, even the most timely, well-crafted pitches might fall through the cracks.
- Organization is everything. Create a spreadsheet to keep track of your story ideas, past pitches, editors' niche beats, your bio, responses – if any – and other useful notes.
- Don't worry about crafting the perfect pitch. Perfection, or your desire to attain it, will likely slow you down. Instead, focus on getting your pitch in good shape; identifying what makes it good, timely, and a fit for the publication you're querying (more on that later); and hit send. A pitch sitting in your inbox draft folder is worthless, right?
- Pitching is a grind. The sooner you accept that, the easier the process will be. But remember, it's a grind that all working writers must endure. Think of it as a rite of passage.

DOI: 10.4324/9781003047629-12

Anatomy of a Pitch

Your pitch should be two to three paragraphs in length. In the subject, write "Pitch: Your Story Idea." Your story idea can be the title of the story you're pitching. Keep it brief.

You can introduce yourself at the beginning of the email by saying you're a freelance writer who covers a particular topic. Then list any past publications and link out to your website. If you're just getting started, you can link out to posts you've published on Medium or your own blog; editors will want to see a work sample if you're hitting them with a cold pitch. Select writing samples similar to the story idea you're pitching. You can also choose to tempt the editor with your idea first and leave your bio to the conclusion of the email.

The meat of your pitch should be one to two paragraphs, written in the style of prose you're intending to tell the story. Explicitly name any sources, experts, reporting you plan to include, and how you intend to pull the story off. Give an estimated word count, add that you're amenable to revisions, and offer fast turnaround (make sure you follow through with this deliverable). Be simple, don't overthink your ideas, and edit for any fluff or filler.

Correctly Identify Your Story

Everyone has ideas. Fewer people have good ideas. But even the best idea won't get published because editors aren't looking for ideas; they're looking for stories. Think about structure: beginning, middle, and end. Consider writing a nut graph, or an outline of the story. Remember, an "exploration" is not a story, no matter how deeply you dive into it. A story is a concrete narrative with reporting, evidence-based data, and insights and typically leaves readers with a takeaway. Once you identify your story, you'll need to find an angle.

Know Your Angle

Think about an angle as your approach to the story. Angles are often what makes a story interesting, unique, and memorable. You'll want to pitch angles that aren't typically covered but are not so obscure there won't be an audience. As you're crafting your angle, think about your audience and why this angle appeals to them. Fashion publications typically have staff cover major fashion events, so when pitching your angle, try to think of something an editor won't have already assigned to an in-house writer. Your angle can make you the perfect person to tell the story. It's essential to convey this information in your pitch.

Research Archival Stories as well as Current Ones

Be sure to check the publication's archives to make sure they haven't published your story idea already. You can check a publication's archives by doing a Google search with the topic keywords and the name of the publication. If the publication has published something similar, you might want to mention that in your pitch, but be sure to explain how your story is different and what it adds to the conversation.

Identify the Right Editor for Your Story Idea

Finding the right editor for your story is part of the heavy lifting required to get your idea off the ground, and it's also essential. How do you find the right editor? Magazine mastheads are a great start. In a digital landscape, Twitter is an amazing resource. Often editors will post on Twitter calling for pitches, so it pays to start following publications; the algorithm will offer suggestions of people to follow. Do that. There are groups on Facebook you can join where writers and editors share resources. The best way to find the right editor is to research the publication thoroughly. If there isn't a masthead or team directory, try LinkedIn, or Google "who is the fashion editor at X publication?".

You might feel like you're on a wild goose chase. Welcome to the world of publishing. It's a fast-paced world filled with swift changes. Editors often change roles or leave publications. Keeping a spreadsheet of contacts – and updating it accordingly – is part of your new job as a pitching journalist, and you can use this to your advantage. Once you've identified some key players, you can follow their social media accounts. Editors typically promote the stories they've worked on or stories they like. Strike up a relationship by leaving comments, and better yet, get a sense of their aesthetic. When you learn their beat, you can pitch editors stories directly geared to their interests.

Identify the Scope and Stakes

Editors are tasked with filling a niche. They want high-stakes stories with a broad scope but not so broad that there's not a clearly defined audience. To make sure your story has scope and stakes, think about the reporting that will go into the story, and make sure you're outlining why you're the perfect person to tell it.

Seduce With the So-What Factor

The so-what factor is what makes the pitch timely. Think about why this story needs to be told now. Also consider that print requires a three-month lead time. Digital stories are typically shorter. If your story is tied to a timely event, specify that in your pitch and use that as the hook. Also mark your pitch as "Time Sensitive Pitch: Your Story Idea" in the subject line of your pitch email. Remember, the so-what factor tells the editor why readers will care. As one of the guidelines provided for submissions by *frankie* says, "The best ideas should be the kind that will make a reader go to their best friend and say, 'You need to see this, it's really inspirational/funny/gut-wrenching/creative/surprising.'"[1]

Nail the Lede, and Wow With Your Prose

The meat of your pitch should include a story lede – the hook – and it should be written in excellent storytelling prose. Imagine this as the first couple of lines of your story. Once you explain the lede, make sure you go on to use compelling and concise prose to outline the rest of your pitch.

Demonstrate How You Will Execute Your Story

If you've done preliminary research, explain your findings. If you've talked to expert sources, explain to whom you've spoken and how their comments will shape the readers' understanding of the story. If your story requires photos or video, explain how you will acquire these or what you already have in hand. If your story requires a product round-up, explain from where you'll draw your sources. In two to three sentences, you should demonstrate to the editor how you're going to pull the story off.

Have a Plan to (Politely) Follow Up

Allow your editor one week before following up with a polite and brief email circling back on the pitch. If you're pitching the editor exclusively, mention that. You can also include a line like, "I'm pitching you exclusively, so if I don't hear back by Friday, I'll assume it's a pass." This is a great technique because it shows your initiative and gives the editor a time frame within which to work. Do not pitch the editor a subsequent story until you've heard back or it's been a couple weeks unless you have a very timely story. But don't be shy about pitching the same editor again and again; writers have been published after six or seven rejected pitches from the same editor.

Where Do You Go From Here?

Throughout *Fashion Writing: A Primer*, we've been providing ideas on where you might publish. Writing for a small, local newspaper can be a good way to learn the ropes of a deadline-driven media, and frequently brands or stores are on the lookout for content providers for their websites or social media accounts. You might even start your own fashion blog where you can showcase your writing. However, at some point, you're going to want to start pitching to outlets with a broader reach (and potentially more pay), but you'll need to have some publication credits under your belt before you do.

There are a number of fashion-focused magazines that actively encourage new writers to submit work. *frankie*, a bimonthly magazine out of Australia, encourages "sharp-eyed perspectives and narratives, bursting with personal insight and wit."[2] They want pitches for stories that aren't what every other magazine publishes. As they say in their submission guidelines, "[I]f you can imagine your idea running in another Australian publication, then you'll have to re-think your pitch." This is an excellent opportunity for fashion writers looking to explore new angles and connections within the fashion world.

Lucy's is a submission-based publication out of the United States and has both a print and an online media presence. Based in Montreal, Canada, *Flanelle Magazine* offers a number of options for publication depending upon the work itself and one's publication needs and even provides a sample pitch letter on their submission page. Other publications friendly to new writers include *London Runway* (out of London, England), which, in addition to standard fashion writing fare, also accepts fiction submissions; *Anon* (based in Milan, Italy); and *BASIC* magazine out of Los Angeles. As we mentioned in the introduction, the landscape for fashion publications is broad, and new magazines are still being launched.

There's one more area to look for opportunities to publish – writing competitions. Publications such as *Vogue* (UK), *Harper's Bazaar* (UK), *TeenVogue*, and *The Sunday Times* have all sponsored writing contests. The work sought ranges from short stories to cultural commentary to memoir.

With time, patience, and persistence, you may very well see your name in print before you know it.

Sample Pitches

A Cold Pitch

SUBJECT: From "Nodel" to Supermodel

Hi Kristen,

I hope this note finds you well. I'm pitching you an exclusive editorial exposé on two emerging supermodels who gained notoriety from Instagram, Richie Shazam and Seashell Cocker.

Street style has evolved. From the pavements to our social feeds, street style's rising stars are reimagining fashion one Instagram post at a time. Fashion is becoming more fluid and self-determined than ever before. But it's still work. In this editorial, with four exclusive hi-res images of Shazam and Seashell (more upon request) by photographer Maya Fuhr, featuring pieces from Lindsay Jones' AW17 MÚSED collection, I interview Shazam and Seashell on their newfound fame in the fashion industry due to social media presence, and the surreal adventures in New York, (like the one photographed) that made them the influencers they are today. Readers will see a slice of summer in New York through their "regal" eyes (mastering the IG game gives them regal status, right?) and the story will capture the "nodel" (a non-model) phenomenon from an inside perspective.

The story will also feature quotes from MÚSED designer Jones, a sculptor, model and former professional muse to such visionaries as Larry Clark, Richard Kern, Richard Prince, and Hugh Hefner – back when Playboy still published nudes. This group of talented players has ethereal edge, making it a perfect fit for R29.

A bit about me: I'm a New York fashion writer whose work has appeared in Vice, Nylon, HuffPost, and more. Because I'm pitching you this story exclusively, if you can get back to me asap, I would kindly appreciate it.

Warm regards,
Fashion Writer
Encl: low-res images: "Summer Regalia"

To an Editor With Pre-Existing Relationship

SUBJECT: Time-Sensitive Pitch: Denim Exhibit Offers Brief History of Blue Jeans & Shows Why They're a Timeless Staple

Hi Erin,

It's been a while since I pitched a story your way, and now I'm pitching a time-sensitive one based on a denim exhibit opening at The Museum of the Fashion Institute of Technology (named one of New York's top ten small museums – and abuzz after its fantastic Susanne Bartsch Fashion Underground show). The new Denim Fashion's Frontier Exhibit opens on Tuesday, 12/1 and runs through May 7, 2016.

Denim is often seen as the ultimate casual cool, a staple of Americana embracing high and low looks. To understand its appeal, you must follow its evolution. A new museum show does just that. My story would cover the opening of the exhibition as well as the show's mission to "explore the multifaceted history of denim and its relationship with high fashion from the 19th century to the present."

My story would highlight some of the 70 objects from the museum's permanent collection, many of which have never been on view. In addition to the history of jeans, Denim will examine a variety of denim garments – from work wear to haute couture.

I will wrap the story with pictures and descriptions of denim women's wear couture from runway collections of Dries Van Noten, Chloë, and Sacaï, as well as menswear pieces from Ralph Lauren and Rag & Bone, all newly acquired pieces by The Museum at FIT.

I have an established relationship with the museum's curator and its head director, Valerie Steele.

This will be a fun piece promoting the exhibit – one of the many great, free fashion events kicking off shopping season in NYC, and celebrating the timelessness of blue jeans. I offer quick turnaround and revisions. Since this is a timely story, if I don't hear from you by EOW*, I'll assume it's a pass.

Warm regards,
Fashion Writer
*EOW means end of week in pitch talk.

What Makes You Different Makes You Great

Fashion Powerhouse Lauren Chan Discusses the Importance of Developing a Niche and Building Community

Lauren Chan is a triple threat – a model, fashion editor, and entrepreneur. A Canadian fashion personality who began her career as a plus-size model, Chan went on to become the fashion features editor at *Glamour* magazine before moving on to launch Henning, her own brand of ethical luxury womenswear for women size 12 and up.

In addition to covering the womenswear market and plus-size fashion beat for *Glamour*, her work has appeared in such publications as *Vogue*, *Interview*, and *The New York Times*' *T Magazine*. Of her accomplishments, the American Society of Magazine Editors said, "Chan is a one-woman multi-media age force for change, raising awareness about size acceptance and body positivity through her work as both an editor [and entrepreneur]."

Can you map the trajectory from graduating from university to where you are now, pointing out moments that changed your direction?

I always wanted to be a fashion editor; after graduating from university, I moved to New York City, where most of the major magazines in North America are based. There, I pursued every opportunity to be part of the fashion industry, whether interning or freelance writing, or by luck, plus-size modelling. When I became a model, I gained access to more of the behind the scenes of the industry and began writing about it. Because of the circumstances, much of my written work became about size-inclusive fashion, and I soon developed a niche. When I later landed as a fashion news editor, I pushed for size-inclusive content across channels (print, digital, social media, product, events, etc.), which solidified my spot as an industry expert in size-inclusive fashion. After some time, I'd done all that I could at the magazine and moved into product with a plus-size clothing brand of my own, Henning. At Henning, writing helps me connect with our customers in many ways – it's a community-building skill I'm grateful to have!

How did your education impact your career path, if it did?

While I wish I'd gone to fashion school, I was able to take a fashion writing class at the University of Western Ontario, which taught me about everything from the business of fashion writing to how to structure a traditional collection review. At the time, I'd been writing for a local blog and the university newspaper, both without much writing guidance – and I didn't have the experience to understand, say, how all the departments of a magazine work together to produce an issue. It (the class) really helped me prepare for the job of a fashion writer in both writing skills and the latent skills needed to work on a fashion media team.

What is one skill that you've found surprisingly important when it comes to fashion writing?

Networking. A lot of my learning about fashion writing was about the skills of a writer. I found that I was missing any education on the business of writing, namely exclusive coverage and/or advertiser/semi-sponsored coverage. Exclusives and advertiser pieces pay the bills at a magazine, so it's important to network with folks on that side of the business in order to secure business.

What connection or community has had the most significant impact on your career?

The community that has had the most impact on my career is the online plus-size fashion community. It's because of their enthusiastic support of my content and brand that I was able to lean into my niche and make an impact in the world of fashion.

When did your love of fashion begin?

I fell in love with fashion after reading the September 2004 issue of *Vogue*. At the time, I was 14 years old, and everything about that issue captured my imagination, from the physical fold-out cover to the profiles of all the models featured on it. From then on, I knew I wanted to be involved in the fashion industry.

What do you see as the function of fashion writing in today's world?

Though it's much less traditional these days – i.e. often in the form of captions – it's exciting that more people are exposed to fashion writing in the form of social media. Social media has certainly made fashion writing more democratic i.e. we don't just listen to the prominent voices at a few select magazines, we listen to accounts like @upnextdesigner.

Does fashion writing have a responsibility to respond to contemporary social issues, and if so, how should it do so?

In my opinion: Absolutely. Fashion is a lens through which we see, create, and reflect on culture. Today, fashion's involvement in racial, gendered, and sizing issues is pivotal in changing the culture to become more inclusive. And – newsflash – it's working.

What is your advice for someone who wants to break into fashion writing?

My advice: develop a niche, find your community, and don't do things the way they've always been done.

What is the best advice, career-wise, that you've been given? How did it impact your path?

The best advice I've received is that what makes you different, makes you great. When I applied that to my work as a fashion journalist, I began writing more about plus-size fashion – at a time where size-inclusive coverage was rare – which set me apart from my peers, solidified my niche, and made me an expert on the topic industry-wide.

What is something an up-and-coming fashion writer should never do?

Ask anything that is Google-able.

Notes

1   "Submissions." *frankie*, www.frankie.com.au/submissions.
2   ditto.

Postgraduate Programmes in Fashion Communication

Listed next are postgraduate-level programmes that offer opportunities to further study fashion communication or fashion journalism. Programmes are organized by country, which are listed alphabetically. Within each country, specific locations are included alphabetically. Following each programme URL, the language coursework is offered in is noted.

Key for languages:

DE – German
CA – Catalan
EN – English
FR – French
IT – Italian
SP – Spanish

Canada

Ontario

Ryerson University

Fashion (MA): www.ryerson.ca/graduate/programs/fashion/
(EN)

France

Paris

American University in Paris

MA in Global Communications, Fashion Track: www.aup.edu/academics/graduate-programs/global-communications/fashion-track
(EN)

India

Pearl Academy (campuses in Delhi-West | Mumbai | Bengaluru | Delhi-South)
PG Professional Diploma in Fashion Communication: pearlacademy.com/academics/courses/postgraduate/fashion-communication/
(EN)

Italy

Florence

IED (Istituto Europeo di Design)

Fashion Business: www.ied.edu/florence/fashion-school/master-courses/fashion-business/CPH2048E
(EN)

Polimoda

Master in Fashion Marketing & Communications: www.polimoda.com/courses/master/fashion-marketing-communications
(EN)

Milan

Accademia Costume & Moda

Fashion Communication & Art Direction: www.accademiacostumeemoda.it/en/programmes/master-fashion-communication-and-art-direction/
(EN)

Accademia del Lusso

Master's degree in Fashion Communication Management: www.accademiadellusso.com/en/courses/masters-courses/fashion-communication-management/
(EN)

Haute Future Fashion Academy

Master's degree in Fashion Promotion & Communication Strategies: www.hffa.it/master-programs/fashion-promotion-communication-strategies
(EN)

IED (Istituto Europeo di Design)

Brand Management and Communication: www.ied.edu/milan/management-school/master-courses/brand-management-and-communication/CPA1786E
(EN and IT)

Fashion Communication and Styling (coursework in English): www.ied.edu/milan/fashion-school/master-courses/fashion-communication-and-styling/MPA1354I
(EN)

Rome

IED (Istituto Europeo di Design)

Comunicazione e Marketing per la Moda: www.ied.edu/rome/fashion-school/master-courses/communication-and-marketing-for-fashion/MPB1845I
(IT)

Mexico

Mexico City

Jannette Klein Universidad

Master's degree in Communication and Digital Dissemination of Fashion: posgrados.jannetteklein.com.mx/maestria-en-comunicacion-y-difusion-digital-de-la-moda/
(SP)

Spain

Barcelona

Blanquerna Universitat Ramon Llul

Master's degree in Fashion Communication: www.blanquerna.edu/en/fcc/masters-and-postgraduate-studies/url-masters/masters-degree-in-fashion-communication
(SP or CA)

Idep Barcelona

Master's degree in Fashion Management & Communication: www.idep.es/estudios/moda/fashion-management-y-comunicacion/
(SP)

Master's degree Styling & Fashion Communication: www.idep.es/estudios/moda/estilismo-y-comunicacion-en-moda/
(SP)

LCI Barcelona

Master in Fashion Marketing, Communication and Event Planning: en.lcibarcelona.com/Diseno-Moda/Master-Marketing-Comunicacion-Organizacion-Eventos-Moda
(EN or SP)

Granada

ESCO Escuela Superior de Comunicación y Marketing de Granada

Master in Fashion: Communication and Management: escogranada.com/masteres/moda/
Online or in-person (SP)

Madrid

IED (Istituto Europeo di Design)

Fashion Styling and Communication: www.ied.edu/madrid/fashion-school/master-courses/fashion-styling-and-communication/CMDMCPE001_01
(EN)
Digital Communication and Marketing in Fashion: www.ied.edu/madrid/fashion-school/master-courses/digital-communication-and-marketing-in-fashion/CMDMCPE0005_01
(EN)

Sabadel

ESDi – Design School

Master's degree in Styling, Image and Fashion Communication: esdi.es/estudios/masters-y-postgrados/master/estilismo-imagen-y-comunicacion-de-moda
(SP)

Valencia

Barreira Arte y Diseño

Master in Communication & Fashion Marketing: barreira.edu.es/moda/master-comunicacion-y-marketing-moda/
(SP)

Switzerland

Lugano

USI Università della Svizzera italiana

Master of Science in Digital Fashion Communication: www.usi.ch/en/education/master/digital-fashion-communication
Double degree with Université Paris 1 Panthéon-Sorbonne
(EN)

United Kingdom

Birmingham

Birmingham City University

Fashion Promotion – MA: www.bcu.ac.uk/courses/fashion-promotion-ma-2022-23
(EN)

Cambridge

Cambridge School of Visual & Performing Arts

MA Fashion: Branding & Creative Communication: www.csvpa.com/art-and-design/ma-fashion-branding-creative-communication/course-details.htm
(EN)

Huddersfield

University of Huddersfield

Fashion Communication and Promotion MA: courses.hud.ac.uk/2022–23/full-time/postgraduate/fashion-communication-and-promotion-ma
(EN)

London

Conde Nast College of Fashion & Design

MA Creative Direction for Fashion Media: https://www.condenastcollege.ac.uk/courses/postgraduate/ma-fashion-media-practice-creative-direction/
(EN)

MA Fashion Communication: www.condenastcollege.ac.uk/courses/postgraduate/ma-fashion-communication/
(EN)

MA Fashion Journalism & Editorial Direction: www.condenastcollege.ac.uk/courses/postgraduate/ma-fashion-media-practice-fashion-journalism-and-editorial-direction/
(EN)

MA Fashion Media Strategy: www.condenastcollege.ac.uk/courses/postgraduate/ma-fashion-media-practice-media-business/
(EN)

UAL: Central Saint Martins

MA Fashion Communication: Fashion Journalism: www.arts.ac.uk/subjects/fashion-communication/postgraduate/ma-fashion-communication-fashion-journalism-csm
(EN)

UAL: London College of Communication

MA Journalism: Arts and Lifestyle Journalism: www.arts.ac.uk/subjects/journalism-pr-media-and-publishing/postgraduate/ma-journalism-arts-and-lifestyle-journalism-lcc
(EN)

UAL: London College of Fashion

MA Fashion Journalism: www.arts.ac.uk/subjects/fashion-communication/postgraduate/ma-fashion-journalism-lcf
(EN)

Nottingham

Nottingham Trent University

Fashion Communications MA: www.ntu.ac.uk/course/art-and-design/pg/this-year/fashion-communications

Fashion Marketing MA: www.ntu.ac.uk/course/art-and-design/pg/ma-fashion-marketing
(EN)

Shoreditch

European College of Business and Management ECBM

Master in International Fashion & Media Management: www.ecbm-london.de/en/master/ma-international-fashion-media-management
Part-time programme (EN & DE)

United States

California

Academy of Art University (San Francisco)

Masters of Arts Program in Fashion Journalism: www.academyart.edu/degree/fashion-journalism/?degree=ma
(EN)

New York

The New School: Parsons School of Design (New York City)

Fashion Studies MA: www.newschool.edu/parsons/ma-fashion-studies/
(EN)

New York University: Gallatin School of Individualized Study (New York City)

MA – Individualized and interdisciplinary programme set by student: gallatin.nyu.edu/academics/graduate.html
(EN)

Online

ELLE Education (in partnership with Complutense University of Madrid, and Mindway Liberal Studies)

Master in Fashion Marketing: elle.education/programs/masters/master-fashion/
(EN)

Index

Note: Page numbers in *italics* indicate a figure and page numbers in **bold** indicate a table on the corresponding page.

Abbey Road 48
accessories 57–58; baguette handbag 57; cloche hat 57; clutch bag 57; fedora 58; fishnet 58; hobo bag 58; minaudiere 58; wristlet 58
acrylic 42
activewear 36
Adam, M. 40
Adichie, C. N. 115, 119
ageism 134
Ahluwalia, P. 107
Aïshti 4
Akil, M. B. 9
Alaïa, A. 14
A-line 38
All About Eve 114
Allure 134
Altman, R. 87
Amed, I. 7
analogous colours 46
Anderson, J. W. 103
androgynous style 36
Annie Hall 21
anorak 32
Apfel, I. 36, 57
appliqué 48
appreciation, cultural 131–132
Arab Spring 112
Aristotle 67
armscye 48
Asos 4
Atkinson, N. 5, 59–65
Atlantic, The 3
Atwood, M. 115
audience 68–70, 117–118; simple versus multiple 69

baguette handbag 57
Balenciaga 84, 121
Balsan, E. 18
bandeau 33
Barber, A. 60
Basque 33
basting 48
batik 48
Battle of Versailles: The Night American Fashion Stumbled Into the Spotlight and Made History, The 119, 121
batwing 41, *41*
BBC Culture 60
Beane, G. 13
Beaton, C. 135
Beckerman, I. 113
Beckett, S. 115
Bedin, G. 17
Behind the Beautiful Forevers: Life, Death, and Hope in a Mumbai Undercity 122
Beker, J. 24
bellow pockets 52, *52*
bell sleeve 41
Benjamin, W. 111
Bérard, C. 19
Bercu, M. 88
Berger, A. 2
Bermuda shorts 33
Beyoncé 14, 83
bias cut 38
Biden, J. 3
bishop sleeve 41
Black Lives Matter 112
black tie 37
Blanks, T. 88, 89, 90, 91–94
blog posts **73**

Blow, I. 81
Boateng, O. 134
boho style 36
bolero 33
Bonner, G. W. 107
Boo, K. 122
Booker, H. 17
bouclé 42
Bowie, D. 91, 99
box pleats 51
brands and content writing 4
Breakfast at Tiffany's 39
British Fashion Council (BFC) 107, 133–134, 136, 137
brocade 42
broderie Anglaise 48
brogues 55, *55*
Broward, C. 15
Brown, M. 85
Browne, T. 85
Bruni, F. 122
Burberry 135
Burke, T. 129
business casual style 36–37
Business of Fashion 7, 91, 94, 139
bustier 33

cable knit 42
camisole 33
Campbell, N. 8, 88, 134
Capel, A. 18
Capri pants 33
cap sleeves 41
capsule collections 58
cargo pocket 52
Carter, E. 104
cartridge pleats 51
Casale, V. 133
cashmere 42–43
Cax, M. 134
Central Saint Martins 97–98
Cerf de Dudzeele, C. 88
cerulean blue 31–32
Chalayan, H. 14, 98
Chambre Syndicale de la Haute Couture 82
Chan, L. 154–156
Chanel 4, 18–19, 42, 44, 81; diversity of models featured by 134; runway shows 84, 87
Chang, J. 115
Chelsea boots 55

chemise 33
Chicago Manual of Style 72
chiffon 43
Chiuri, M. G. 19
chunking 71
cigarette pant 33
cloche hat 57
clutch bag 57
CNN Style 60
Cocteau, J. 19
cold pitch 152–153
collaborators, runway show 87–88
colour(s) 31–32; analogous 46; complimentary 46; hue 46; nude as a 132–133; primary 46; saturation of 47; secondary 47; shade 47; tertiary 47; tint 47; trend reports 100; value of 47
Comme des Garçons 21–22, 37, 87
complimentary colours 46
cone heel 56
Confessions of a Shopaholic 114
conspicuous consumption 14
Consumed: The Need for Collective Change: Colonialism, Climate Change & Consumerism 60
contemporary issues in fashion 129–130; appreciation versus appropriation 131–132; cultural appropriation 130–131; diversity and inclusion 132–135; social justice movements 14, 112, 129–130; sustainability 68, 107, 114, 135–137; writing about 138; writing without bias on 138–139
content marketing 4
context of runway shows 86
Corset: A Cultural History, The 97
corsets 34, 96–97
Costa, F. 21
Council of Fashion Designers of America (CFDA) 133, 137
Coveteur 6
COVID-19 pandemic 7, 15, 62, 100
cowl neckline 40
Craft of Use: Post-Growth Fashion 114
Crayola 133
creative nonfiction 113
cruise collections 58; runway shows 83
culottes 34, *34*
cultural appropriation 130–131; versus appreciation 131–132
Cunningham, B. 13
Cunningham, M. 22
Cut, The 7

Daily Beast, The 119
Daily Express 75
Daily Telegraph, The 104
Daley, N. 107
Dalí, S. 19
Dapper Dan 22–23
darts 49
David Bowie Is 99
Day, D. 22–23
de Beauharnais, J. 38
Delevigne, C. 88
Deliverance 1
Dell'Orifice, C. 135
Details 13
Detroit Free Press, The 119
Devil Wears Prada, The 31–32, 114
Dhaka garment factory collapse 135–136
Diana, Princess 22
Dictionary of Costume and Fashion, A 64
Diet Prada 4
digital fashion writing 3–4, 71–72, **73–74**
Dior 4; New Look 19, 20, 24, 37, 38, *38*, 81; runway shows 87, 88
Dior, C. 19, 37, 55
disabled models 134
distressed areas 49
diversity and inclusion in fashion 132–135
Dixon, D. 23
Dolman sleeve 41
Doré, G. 113
D'Orsay shoe 56
drape 49
Dressed: The History of Fashion 13
Dress for Success 22
duffle coat 34

'80s power dressing 22
Elbaz, A. 104, 143
Elle 2, 84, 117
Elle India 139, 140
Ellis, P. 21
Ellis-Ross, T. 83
Elson, K. 88
embroidery 49
empire line 38
environmentalism 14
epaulets 49
Ephron, D. 113
Ephron, N. 113
Erdem 103
espadrille 56
ethos 68
Eugenie of France, empress 39

European Literature Network 115
Evaristo, B. 115
Everlane 137
Every Outfit on Sex & the City 4
Exquisite Magazine 3
eyelets 49

fabrics 42–46; acrylic 42; bouclé 42; brocade 42; cable knit 542; cashmere 42–43; chiffon 43; gingham 43; herringbone 43, *43*; houndstooth 43; jacquard 43–44; jersey 44; lamé 44; Merino wool 44; mohair 44; opaque 44; pile 44; plaid 44; satin 44; seersucker 45, *45*; shirting 45; spandex 45; suiting 45; tulle 45; velour 45–46; velvet 46; wool 56
Face, The 75
Fall/Winter runway shows 82
Fantastic Man 72, 91
fashion:'80s power dressing 22; brief history of 13–15; conspicuous consumption and 14; cultural appropriation in 130–132; diversity and inclusion in 132–135; in films and television 21, 87, 113; Industrial Revolution and 15–16; language of (*See* language of fashion); Orientalism and 17; politics and 2, 14–15; Saville Row 47–48; slow 136; as spectacle 81–82; sustainability in 68, 107, 114, 135–137; technological advances and 15; television journalists and 24–27; youth subculture and 20
Fashion (Broward) 15
Fashion (magazine) 60
Fashion and Race Database 110–111
Fashion Colour Trend Report 100
fashion designers: Calvin Klein 21; Charles Frederick Worth 16–17; Christian Dior 4, 19; Coco Chanel 4, 18–19; Dapper Dan 22–23; earliest 15–16; James Jebbia 23–24; Mary Quant 19–20; Paul Poiret 13, 17–18; Rei Kawakubo 14, 21–22
Fashion Designers Association of Nigeria (FADAN) 137
Fashion Designers from A to Z 13
Fashion File 91, 94
Fashioning Masculinities: The Art of Menswear 72, 83
Fashion Is Spinach 64
Fashion Revolution 136
Fashion Television 24, 25, 26
Fashion Theory 117

Fashion Victims: The Dangers of Dress Past and Present 116
fashion writers: Amanda Winnie Kabuiku 6–9; Bandana Tewari 139–144; Charlie Porter 72–83; diverse skills of 115–116; Jeanne Beker 24–27; Lauren Chan 154–156; Nathalie Atkinson 59–65; organizing thoughts and writing about runway shows 89; pitching process (*See* pitching process); podcasts of 116–117; Robin Givhan 6, 62, 88, 118–123; at runway shows 88–89; Sarah Mower 1–2, 82, 86, 88, 103–108; Suzy Menkes 5, 88, 89, 90, 116, 143; Tim Blanks 88, 89, 90, 91–94
fashion writing: changing landscapes of 4–5; content marketing 4; defined 2; digital 3–4, 71–72, **73–74**; feature pieces (*see* feature writing); as genre 1; knowing the audience for 68–70, 117–118; online 3–4; politics and 2; postgraduate programmes in 157–163; in print 2–3; with purpose 67–68; reports versus reviews 90–91; on runway shows (*See* runway shows); style guides for 72; trend reports (*See* trend reports); trustworthiness in 69; writer-based prose versus reader-based prose in 70–71
feature writing 110–111; audience for 112–113; as creative nonfiction 113; diverse skills of writers of 115–116; organization of 112–113; podcasts and 116–117; process of 117–118; protest movements and 112; research in 112; stories told through 114–115; structure of 111–112
Fédération de la Haute Couture et de la Mode (FHCM) 137
fedora 58
Fendi 23; diversity of models featured by 134
Fenty 135
filigree 49
films and television 21, 87, 113
Financial Times, The 91
first look at runway shows 85
fishnet 58
fishtail 38
fit and flare 38, *38*
Flanelle Magazine 152
Fletcher, K. 114
Flower, L. S. 70
Floyd, G. 7

fluted hem 39
footwear 55–58; brogue 55, *55*; Chelsea boots 55; cone heel 56; D'Orsay shoe 56; espadrille 56; gladiator sandal 56; loafer 56; Mary Jane 56; mule 56; Oxford 56–57; slide 57; stiletto heels 57; wedge heels 57
Ford, Tanisha C. 64
Ford, Tom 88
formal wear 37
FQ: Fashion Quarterly 24
Fraser, K. 64
Fresh Dressed 23

Galliano, J. 19, 27, 87
garments 32–36; anorak 32; bandeau 33; Basque 33; Bermuda shorts 33; bolero 33; camisole 33; Capri pants 33; chemise 33; cigarette pant 33; corset 34, 96–97; culottes 34, *34*; duffle coat 34; gaucho 34; halter 34; harem pants 34; hobble skirt 35; jodhpurs 35; maxi 35; micromini 35; miniskirt 35; polo neck 35; tunic 35; turtleneck 35; unitard 35; waistcoat 36
Garner, E. 85
gathers 49
gaucho 34
Gaultier, J. P. 104
Gayten, B. 19
Gerber, K. J. 88
German Fashion Designers Foundation (GFDF) 137
Gevinson, T. 26
Gibson, W. 5–6, 115
gig economy 4
Gill, A. A. 63
gingham 43
Giorgio Armani 13
Givhan, R. 6, 62, 88, 118–123
gladiator sandal 56
Glamour 3, 6, 154
Global Garbs 3
Globe and Mail, The 24, 26, 59–60, *60*, 62–63
godet pleats 50, *50*, 52
gore inserts 50
GQ 91
grammar 72
Guardian, The 3, 72, 74, 76, 103
Gucci 23, 81, 140
guests lists, runway show 83–84

Guide to Sustainable Strategies, CFDA 137
gussets 50

Hadid, G. 88
Halston 21
halter 34
Hamnet, K. 14
handkerchief hem 39
harem pants 34
Harlow, S. 85
Harper's Bazaar UK 152
Harper's Bazaar US 81, 84, 103
haute couture 59; runway shows 82
Hawes, E. 64
Hearst, G. 107
hems 39
Henry VIII, King 53
Hepburn, A. 39
herringbone 43, *43*
H&M 4
hobble skirt 35
hobo bag 58
Hong Kong Fashion Designers Association (HKFDA) 137
Horyn, C. 88
houndstooth 43
hue 46
HuffPost 3

Idle No More 112
i-D Vice France 6
Independent 76
Industrial Revolution 15–16
Instagram 4, 71, **73**, 135
Interview 91, 154
Iribe, P. 17

Jacobs, M. 81, 84, 85, 87
jacquard 43–44
Jacquard, J.-M. 44
James, R. 48
J. Crew 2
Jean-Raymond, K. 85, 107
Jebbia, J. 23–24
jersey 44
J-Lo 83
jodhpurs 35
Joe Fresh 135
Johnson, B. 134
Johnson, J. 134–135

Kabuiku, A. W. 6–9
kangaroo pockets 52
Karan, D. 37, 58, 100

Kawakubo, R. 14, 21–22, 87, 91
Keaton, D. 21, 83
Kendi, I. X. 122
Kent, N. 91
keyhole neckline 40
kick pleats 52
Killer Style: How Fashion Has Injured, Maimed, & Murdered Through History 116
Kimono: From Kyoto to Catwalk 99
Klein, C. 21, 37
Klensch, E. 25
knife pleat 52
Knockoff, The 114
Kors, M. 37
Kruger, B. 23
Kurihara, T. 22

Lacroix, C. 14, 27
Lagerfeld, K. 19, 26, 27, 81, 87, 134, 141–142
lamé 44
language of fashion 30–32; about colour 31–32, 46–47; about elements to highlight 30–31; about garments 32–36; about outfits 30; about silhouettes 37–42; about style 36–37; accessories 57–58; bustier 33; fabrics 42–46; footwear 55–57; general terms 58–59; tailoring terms and techniques 47–55
lapel 50
Lau, S. 5
Lauren, G. 107
Lauren, R. 21
Le Monde Afrique 6
Liberated Threads: Black Women, Style, and the Global Politics of Soul 64
line (garment) 59
little black dress (LDB) 44
Livingston, D. 64
loafer 56
logos 67
London Runway 152
look books 59
Loro Piana 137
Louis Vuitton 23, 81, 84, 87, 140; runway shows 85
Louis XIV, King 15
Love 3
Love, Loss, and What I Wore 6, 113
Love Style Life 113
Lucky 61
Lucy's 152
Luna, D. 134

MacDonald, I. 91
Madewell 4
Madonna 97
Mahon, S.-M. 115–116
Maison Margiela 87
makeup artists, runway show 88
Mandarin collar 40, *40*
Mango 135
Margiela, M. 104
Marie Claire 114
Marilyn, M. 107
Mary Jane shoe 56
maxi 35
maxitrends *101*
Mayer, A. 111
McCardell, C. 37
McCartney, S. 14, 98, 107
McGrath, P. 88
McQueen, A. 1–2, 14, 27, 76, 81, 91; diversity of models featured by 134; runway shows 85, 87; trend spotting and 97–98, 99
megatrends *101*
Menkes, S. 5, 88, 89, 90, 116, 143
Mercado, J. 134
Merino wool 44
#MeToo movement 129–130
Michele, A. 81
micromini 35
microtrends 101, *101*
millinery 59
minaudiere bag 58
miniskirt 35
Miyake, I. 22
Mizrahi, I. 13
MLA Style Manual 72
M le Monde 7
models, runway show 88; diverse 134–135
Modern Language Association 72
mohair 44
Mohamed, R. 134
Molloy, J. T. 22
Moss, K. 21
Moss, P. 85, 134
Mower, S. 1–2, 82, 86, 88, 103–108
Ms London 103, 105
Mukwege, D. 130
mule 56
multiple audiences 69
Murad, N. 130
Murray, C. S. 91
music, runway show 85

Naïfs 6, 7, 8
Napoleon 38

National Post 62
neckline 40
Net-a-Porter 4
Newhouse, J. 143
New Look 19, 20, 24, 37, 38, *38*, 81
New Music, The 25
New Yorker, The 64, 122
New York Magazine 61, 119
New York Observer 113
New York Times 13, 76, 100, 122, 154
New York Times Sunday Review 132
Nicholson, A. 134
Nu, Y. 134
nude as a colour 132–133
Nutter, T. 48

Oates, J. C. 122
Obama, M. 2, 119
O de l'Obs 7
ombré 50
online fashion writing *see* digital fashion writing
opaque fabric 44
Orientalism 17
overlay 50
Oxford shoe 56–57

Page, D. 88
Pantone 100, 132–133
paper bag waistband 41–42
Parker, S. J. 84, 113
Parton, D. 100
Patagonia 137
patch pockets 52, *52*
patchwork 50
pathos 68
Pecheux, T. 88
peek-a-boo 51
peplum 51, *51*
Perkin, W. 61
persuasive writing 67–68
Peter Pan collar 40
Piazza, J. 114
Pickens, M. B. 64
pile 44
piping 51
pitching process 148; anatomy of pitch in 149; to an editor with pre-existing relationship 153; angle to 149; cold pitch 152–153; correctly identifying your story in 149; demonstrating how you'll execute your story in 151; having a plan to (politely) follow-up in 151; identifying the right editor in 150; identifying the scope and stakes in

150; looking for new opportunities in 151–152; researching archival stories as well as current ones in 149–150; seducing with the so-what factor in 150; story lede in 151
placket 52
plaid 44
pleats 50, 50, 51–52
pockets 52–53, 52
podcasts 116–117
Poiret, P. 13, 17–18, 34, 81
politics and fashion 2, 14–15
Pollack, S. 1
Pollock, G. 105
polo neck 35
Porter, C. 72–83
Positive Fashion Initiative 136
postgraduate programmes in fashion communication 157–163
power dressing 22
Prada 135
pre-fall runway shows 83
pret-a-porter 59
Prêt-à-Porter 87
Primark 135
primary colour 46
princess line 39
print fashion writing 2–3
Proenza Schouler show 84
protests movements 14, 108, 112
Pucci, E. 33
puffed sleeve 42
punctuation 72
purpose, writing with 67–68

Quant, M. 19–20
Quant by Quant 19–20
quilting 53

raglan 53
reader-based prose 70–71
Reboux, C. 57
Reese, T. 2
Refinery29 63
Renaissance 3
resort wear 37; runway shows 83
ribbing 53
Rihanna 134–135
Rocha, S. 103
Roots of Style: Weaving Together Life, Love, and Fashion 113
ruching 53
ruffle 53

runway shows: clothes at 85–86; collaborators of 87–88; context of 86; environment and sets at 84–85; Fall/Winter 82; fashion as spectacle and 81–82; first look at 85; guests lists 83–84; haute couture 82; makeup artists at 88; models at 88, 134; organizing thoughts and writing reports on 89; past, present, and future of 87; pre-fall 83; reporters at 88–89; reports versus reviews of 90–91; resort or cruise 83; sounds at 85; Spring/Summer 83; stylists at 88; as theatre 84–85; what to look for at 83–89
Rushdie, S. 115

Said, E. 17, 130
Saint Laurent, Y. 38, 39, 82; runway shows 84, 88
Sardone, A. 60
sartorial (style) 59
satin 44
saturation 47
Saunders, B. 107
Savage Beauty 99
Saville Row 47–48
scalloped technique 53
Schiaparelli, E. 54
Schulman, S. 61
Scott, J. 86
Sears *Wish Book* 6
secondary colour 47
seersucker 45, 45
Selfe, D. 135
Semaan, C. 107
service pieces 103, 110
Sex & the City 113
shade 47
Shafak, E. 115
sheath 39
Sheep Inc. 137
Sherman, C. 72
shibori 53
Shields, B. 21
shift 39
shirting 45
silhouettes 37–42; A-line 38; bias cut 38; empire line 38; fishtail 38; fit and flare 38, 38; hems 39; neckline 40; princess line 39; sheath 39; shift 39; sleeves 41–42, 41; tea length 39; trapeze line 39; X-line 39
Simons, R. 19

simple audiences 69
sleeves 41–42, *41*
slide shoe 57
Slimane, H. 81
Slone, A. 24–27
slow fashion 6, 136
smart casual style 36–37
social justice 14, 124
social media 4, 71, **73–74**, 133; podcasts and 116–117; protest movements and 112; trend spotting on 98
social movements 14, 112, 129–130
Sotomayor, S. 23
soutache braid 54
spaghetti strap 54
spandex 45
spangles 54
sportswear 37
Spring/Summer runway shows 83
SSense 4
Stamped From the Beginning 122
Stewart, M. 63
stiletto heels 57
Stone, S. 99
storyboarding 71
story lede 151
Streep, M. 111
streetwear 37
Stüssy 23, 37
Stussy, S. 23
style 36–37; activewear 36; androgynous 36; boho 36; business casual 36–37; formal wear 37; resort wear 37; sportswear 37; streetwear 37
style.com 94
style guides 72
StyleLikeU 134
Style Out There 132
Style Rookie 26
stylists, runway show 88
subcultures 20
Substack **73**
Sui, A. 88
suiting 45
Sunday Times, The 152
Supreme 23–24, 37
sustainability in fashion 68, 107, 114, 135–137
sweetheart neckline 40
Sykes, L. 114

tailoring terms and techniques 47–55; appliqué 48; armscye 48; basting 48; batik 48; broderie Anglaise 48; dart 49; distressed 49; drape 49; embroidery 49; epaulet 49; eyelets 49; filigree 49; gathers 49; godet pleats 50, *50*, 52; gore 50; gusset 50; lapel 50; ombré 50; overlay 50; patchwork 50; peek-a-boo 51; peplum 51, *51*; piping 51; placket 51; pleat 51–52; pocket 52–53; quilting 53; raglan 53; ribbing 53; ruching 53; ruffle 53; scalloped technique 53; shibori 53; soutache braid 54; spaghetti strap 54; spangles 54; tie dye 54; trompe l'oeil 54; tuck 54; yoke 54–55
Takahashi, J. 22
Taschen 13
Taylor, G. 2
tea length 39
technological advances and fashion 15
TeenVogue 131, 134, 152
television journalists and fashion 24–27
Tennant, S. 88
tertiary colour 47
Tewari, B. 139–144
Thatcher, M. 22, 111
theatre, runway shows as 84–85
Theory of the Leisure Class, The 14
They Shoot Horses, Don't They? 1
Thunberg, G. 134
tie dye 54
Tiffany & Co. 4
TikTok 71, **74**
Times of India 140
Times UK 63, 103
tint 47
T Magazine 7, 154
Toledo, I. 113
Tom Ford 89
Toronto Life Fashion 94
trapeze line 39
trend reports 96; catchy names in 101; colour 100; defined 96; on microtrends 101; service pieces and 103; on specific looks 99–100; thematic lens of 100–101; trend pyramid *101*; trend spotting and 97–99; writing 102–103
trend spotting 97–99
trompe l'oeil 54
trophy items 100
Trudeau, J. 2
tuck 54
tulle 45
tunic 35
turtleneck 35

Twitter **74**, 133
Type Books 116

Ukraine war 9
Underground Railroad, The 122
unitard 35
United Fashion 137
United Nations Alliance for Sustainable Fashion 136

Valli, G. 37
value, colour or hue 47
Van Herpen, I. 37
Van Noten, D. 7
Veblen, T. 14
velour 45–46
velvet 46
Versace 4
Vetements show 83–84
Viard, V. 19
Village Voice 62
Vionnet, M. 38
Vogue 2, 6, 134, 154; audience of 68; Charlie Porter and 75; diversity of models featured by 134–135; Robin Givhan and 119; runway shows and 84; Sarah Mower and 103, 104, 105; stylists at 88; Tim Blanks and 91
Vogue Australia 70
Vogue India 139–141
Vogue Paris 134
Vogue Scandinavia 134
Vogue UK 31, 134, 152
Vreeland, D. 91
Vulture 60

Wagner, L. P. 7
Wahlberg, M. 21
waistcoat 36
Waiting for Godot 115
Wang, C. 132
Warhol, A. 72

Warren, A. 133
Washington Post, The 62, 118–119, 122
Waste and Resources Action Plan (WRAP) 129
Watanabe, J. 22
wedge heels 57
welt pockets 53
Werner, C. 134
Westman, G. 88
Westwood, V. 14
What Artists Wear 72
Whitehead, C. 122
white tie 37
Wild Dress: Clothing & the Natural World 114
Williams, R. 20, 91
wing collar 40
Wintour, A. 83
Women: Dress for Success 22
Women in Clothes 114
wool 46
Worn Fashion Journal 115–116
Worn Stories 114
Worth, C. F. 16–17, 39, 59, 81
wristlet 58
Writer-Based Prose: A Cognitive Basis for Problems in Writing 70
Wu, J. 2

Xi Jinping 2
X-line 39

Yaeger, L. 5, 62
Yamamoto, Y. 22
Yin, Y. 18
yoke 54–55
youth subculture 20
YouTube 4

Zero History 5–6, 115
Zhao, C. 99

For Product Safety Concerns and Information please contact our EU
representative GPSR@taylorandfrancis.com
Taylor & Francis Verlag GmbH, Kaufingerstraße 24, 80331 München, Germany

www.ingramcontent.com/pod-product-compliance
Lightning Source LLC
Chambersburg PA
CBHW051400290426
44108CB00015B/2089